Jews
of the
South

Selected Essays from the
Southern Jewish Historical Society

edited by
Samuel Proctor and Louis Schmier
with
Malcolm Stern

ISBN 0-86554-102-7

All books published by Mercer University Press are produced
on acid-free paper that exceeds the minimum standards set by
the National Historical Publications and Records Commission.

Library of Congress of Cataloging in Publication Data:

Jews of the South

 Contents: Jews and Gentiles in a south Georgia town / by Louis Schmier —
Moses Elias Levy and attempts to colonize Florida / by Joseph Gary Adler — Penina Moise, southern Jewish poetess / by Solomon Breibart — [etc.]

 1. Jews—Southern States—History—Addresses, essays, lectures. 2. Southern
States—Ethnic relations—Addresses, essays, lectures. I. Proctor, Samuel. II.
Schmier, Louis, 1940-   . III. Stern, Malcolm H. IV. Southern Jewish Historical
Society (U.S.)
F220.J5J48 1984   975'.004924   83-25060
ISBN 0-86554-102-7 (alk. paper)

Contents

Foreword

One of the most remarkable manifestations in world Jewish history is the emergence of the American Jewish community. Before World War II, there was only one American Jewish historical society in the whole land; this was a national organization housed in two rooms on the premises of a New York rabbinical seminary. Today there are several national societies and well over twenty local American Jewish historical associations, organizations stretching all the way from New England to Southern California. This almost startling efflorescence—really an explosion!—is due to the fact that American Jewry now exercises a significant measure of spiritual and cultural hegemony over world Jewry in almost every sphere of endeavor. American Jewish historical societies, museums, and synagogal archives have begun to dot the South and the new Southwest; the Southern Jewish Historical Society is one striking example.

Jews everywhere—and certainly in the South—are increasingly aware of the early origins of Jewish life in the United States. This volume of essays to which I am privileged to preface a few words helps document the fact that Jews have been pioneers in the states of the South. Ever since the mid-seventeenth century they have participated in virtually every aspect of life and struggles of the Southern region. They were active as plantation owners, ranchers, small farmers, journalists, urban businessmen—and business-women too—as political rebels, soldiers, and statesmen. Mrs. Solomon Cohen, of Savannah, lived to see thirty-two of her descendants enlist in the armed forces of the Confederacy. One of them, Abraham C. Myers, was the new government's quartermaster general. His Jewish associates included the Confederacy's first surgeon general, David Camden De Leon, and its secretary of war and of state, the brilliant, enigmatic Judah P. Benjamin.

These essays, now published by the Southern Jewish Historical Society, offer data certain to throw light on the Revolution in Georgia, on the Florida colonization plans of Moses Elias Levy, on the life of that brave and kindly poet, Penina Moise, daughter of refugees who had fled the terrors of slave revolts in the Caribbean islands. It is good to note that recognition is now being accorded Philip Phillips, one of the greatest lawyers ever to argue a case before the United States Supreme Court. Dr. Bernard C. Ehrenreich is given a well-deserved place in history; I remember him when, as an infantryman in the 37th Ohio Division during World War I, I first met this charming, courteous gentleman who, I later discovered, was among the country's early Zionists. Ludwig Lewisohn is not ignored in this volume. Here was a litterateur of superb quality; it is sad that the times were unkind to him. One may venture the hope that, as the decades pass, his stature will loom ever larger.

As all of these essays demonstrate, Southern Jews were an integral part of the history of the region in which they dwelt and which, in general, made them welcome. They are important, too, for the history of the Jews in the country as a whole. Charleston, up to 1820, was the largest Jewish community in the United States and certainly the most cultured in the secular sense. The questions the historian now poses are these: is there a special Southern Jewish regional history, a distinctive Southern Jewish psyche, mind-set, ethos? In a larger sense, is the South really different from the North? These essays may help us find the answers.

American Jewish Archives   Jacob R. Marcus

1

Jews and Gentiles in a South Georgia Town

by Louis Schmier

At the beginning of the twentieth century, Margaret Varnedoe, one of the prominent young Gentile women of Valdosta society, was reminiscing of her youth with her daughter, Julia. Among the people she mentioned were the families of George Ehrlich and Emanuel Engel, who were among the first Jews to settle in Valdosta. "They were good people," she told her daughter, "and everyone liked them." She had especially warm memories of George Ehrlich's younger son, Henry, who had courted her for a time. And then, in passing, she added pridefully, "Why, they became like one of us."

"They must have been different Jews," thought Julia to herself, "and not like the Jews on Nigger Street. Why you can't hardly understand a word they say. Those Ehrlichs must have been Jews like the Markses. Sam is always in plays and things people are putting on; and he's always singing in church; and Sadie is always at every party with all the boys around her."[1]

---

[1]Interview with Mrs. Lloyd Greer (Valdosta GA), 9 December 1976. All tapes and transcripts of interviews cited are in the possession of the author.

This scene is a table of contents for the story of the relationships that developed between Jews and non-Jews in Valdosta from 1866 until the beginning of World War II. The opening chapters, which deal solely with the German Jews, unfold in an almost relaxed atmosphere heavily influenced both by Valdosta's short history and the character of its first Jewish settlers.

Valdosta, located some 160 miles southwest of Savannah, was founded in 1860. The Civil War had come too early, however, for the Valdostans to have had the opportunity to develop the hierarchical system that typified Southern white society, at the bottom of which any newly arrived Jews would have been placed. In March 1866, as Valdosta was recovering from the hardships of war and experiencing a virtual refounding, Bernard Kaul and Abraham Ehrlich arrived. They were soon followed by Abraham's brothers, cousins, and his uncle George.[2]

The Gentile response to their presence was a receptive one for several reasons. Not least was the fact that these Jews were not strangers to the Valdostans. George Ehrlich, sometimes accompanied by Abraham or his son, Michael, had peddled this area throughout the late 1850s. Moreover, during the war he had sent his family to Valdosta to escape possible harm from Federal naval shelling of Savannah. Economic considerations were an added inducement for the Gentiles to accept the Jewish arrival, for in the period after the war, when merchants and commodities were scarce, the Ehrlichs, with their Savannah "connections," were greeted as significant contributors to the revival of the town.[3]

There were some natives, however, who reminded the townspeople of the reasons for nearby Thomasville's explusion of its few Jews in 1862. They warned that the Jews would also try to exploit Valdosta's economic plight to their own advantage. In response to such comments, the editor of the local newspaper argued that the Ehrlichs were proper representatives of those white German im-

---

[2]For the activities of the German Jews in Valdosta, see Louis Schmier, "The First Jews of Valdosta," *Georgia Historical Quarterly* 62 (Spring 1978): 32-49; "The Man from Gehau," *Atlanta Historical Quarterly* 23 (Fall 1979): 91-106.

[3]Thannie Smith Wisenbaker, "First Impressions of Valdosta in 1863" (unpublished memoir in the possession of Mrs. Susan McKey Thomas, Valdosta GA) 14.

migrants the local townspeople were seeking when they formed the Immigration Society to stem the trends of "spreading niggerism."[4]

In a society where the only social distinction had been drawn according to racial lines, the special status of the freedmen, not the presence of a few white Jews who had once owned slaves themselves, was seen as the real threat to the basic stability of Valdosta. In issue after issue the local newspaper editor wrote angrily against the "irresponsibility of the freedman" and the burden he imposed on white society. Such social sins were often contrasted with the social virtues of the Jews: that the Jews "are noted for kindness to their own people"; that they "do not let their poor come upon the public"; and that "they care for widows and orphans."[5]

The emphasis of these comments, however, was more a condemnation of the special treatment given to the freedman than praise for the Jew. By picturing the Jews as the lesser of two evils, the newspaper revealed that however receptive the Valdostans might have been to the idea of Jews living among them, inwardly they were not ready to put aside their prejudices. The Jews, therefore, were only too happy to let the freedmen act as a social lightning rod absorbing bolts of animosity that might otherwise have struck them. "My grandmother used to say," affirmed an Ehrlich descendant, "too long it was us. Now it is their turn. Better it should be that way."[6] The presence of the blacks, therefore, gave the Jews a greater sense of security and freedom.

The need for a buffer was deeply rooted in the haunting sense of difference that pervaded the thinking of both Jew and Gentile. Articles appeared in the local newspaper discussing Jewish customs in terms that referred to traditional stereotypes and seemingly promoted a theme of Jewish aloofness and separateness. Yet while such pieces kept these Jews on their guard, they were never written with malice or in a provocative tone that might have catalyzed word into action. Rather, they were items of information de-

---

[4]*South Georgia Times*, 15 April 1868.

[5]Ibid., 22, 29 April 1868.

[6]Interview with Claire Friedman (Savannah GA), 16 December 1975.

signed to satisfy Gentiles' curiosity about local Jews who were becoming increasingly prominent. Indeed, some articles were conciliatory: "The Jewish nose is full of character. It is always in keeping with the face," wrote an editor in 1879. This statement was followed by a left-handed compliment that described the Jewish nose as a better nose than the "lazy" and "not fine African nose."[7] Other articles tended to deemphasize differences between Jews and Gentiles: "The rite of circumcision," explained an editor in 1875, is "a Jewish ordinance that corresponds with baptism of Christians."[8] Still other stereotypes were balanced by countervailing ones. The Jews were Christ-killers, but they were also "servants of God without whom progress would be unreal and civilization unstable."[9] They might use devious economic practices, but they were shrewd businessmen to be admired. They often married for money, but they had a strong sense of family. The Jews might be sojourners in a strange land, but they hated Ulysses S. Grant, and any enemy of Grant was a friend of the South.[10]

The number of such articles were few, numbering no more than fifteen between 1866 and 1890. Most were written in the 1870s, and none after 1889. As the Valdostans knew more about Jews from their own personal contacts, they relied less on the uncomplimentary stereotypes as standards by which to judge the actions of their neighbors. Other credentials of the German Jews hastened this process. Of importance was the fact that Abraham Ehrlich and Bernard Kaul were Confederate veterans.[11] One glance at Abraham

---

[7]Valdosta *Times*, 24 May 1879.

[8]Ibid., 11 September 1875.

[9]Ibid., 19 December 1885; 25 June 1887.

[10]*South Georgia Times*, 15 April 1868; Valdosta *Times*, 11, 17 November; 19 December 1885; 10 March 1887; Quitman *Banner*, 8 January 1869.

[11]Abraham Ehrlich had fought at Vicksburg and Chickamauga with the Georgia Sharpshooters, while Bernard Kaul was in Lee's Army of Virginia in the Eighth Florida Regiment. See Abraham Ehrlich, Compiled Service Records of Confederate Soldiers Who Served in Organizations from the State of Georgia, National Archives microfilm no. 266, roll 196; Benjamin Kaul, Compiled Service Records of Soldiers Who Served in Organizations from the State of Florida, National Archives microfilm no. M-251, roll 83.

Ehrlich's arm, withered by a Union minié ball at Chickamauga, convinced the Gentiles of Valdosta that among them were Jews who had helped defend the South against the desecration of its soil and the deprivation of its liberty. In the post-Civil War South, glorifying its past and honoring its struggle was an important recommendation for acceptance and admiration.[12]

Equally significant was the fact that while the Jews did not hide from their cultural heritage, and often stood up in its defense, they did not flaunt it. George Ehrlich, in particular, was an "Americanized Jew." From the time he arrived in the United States in the 1830s, he began shedding many outward cultural differences in order to be like the Gentile majority. To the Valdosta Gentiles this attempt was most evident in George's use of such "Christian" names as Ambrose for his children.[13] Fighting shoulder to shoulder with the Gentiles rather than against them and living away from their own kind for the first time were experiences for Abraham Ehrlich and Bernard Kaul in which they learned the lessons and rewards of conformity. After the war, finding it easier to be a part of the Gentile world than separated from it, these Jews became increasingly easygoing toward ritual observances that had a visible segregating effect. This process moved at a still quicker pace in Valdosta, whose small-town environment demanded a natural modification in the ritual observance.[14]

---

[12]On the occasion of Abraham Ehrlich's death in July 1870, a number of obituaries appeared in local newspapers. "A. A. Ehrlich [gave] his life to a cause five years after that cause was lost. Thus remember him each year with scattered flowers on the graves of our immortal loved and lost," wrote the Savannah *Republican* on 6 July 1870. On 9 July 1870, the Bainbridge *Argus* wrote: "That he was true and brave and patriotic we need no better proof than his death, which was caused by his wounds while defending the rights and liberties of his struggling country. All honor to his memory."

[13]Valdosta *Times*, 27 October 1888.

[14]Interview with Jane Strauss (New York NY), 12 December 1975; interview with Anne Solomon (Savannah GA), 17 December 1975. High-holiday services were being held in the surrounding towns of Quitman and Thomasville, but the Jews in Valdosta made no apparent effort to participate. See Quitman *Banner*, 5 May 1878; Mickve Israel Synagogue (Savannah GA) Minute Book 1852-1888, 14 September 1879, 19 February 1880, Georgia Historical Society, Savannah, Georgia.

The immigrant parents, with their memories of Europe, were more sensitive to Gentile attitudes; their Southern-born children had a more casual approach to the situation. They thought of themselves more as Southerners who were Jewish than Jews who lived in the South. They could find few signs of social ostracism, economic harassment, or political discrimination. To be sure, Emanuel Engel had caused a sensation in 1874, when two weeks after arriving in Valdosta he had married Susan Allen, one of the Gentile belles. But the subsequent action taken by the Gentiles was merely a temporary social banishment of the couple.[15] And because the other Jews remained unaffected, they treated the Gentile response as an isolated and understandable reaction not symptomatic of a general malaise. Consequently, these Jews were concerned less with proving that they were "good Jews" than displaying their civic-mindedness and social respectability.

For their part, the Valdosta Gentiles were ready to take them at their word. These Jews attended social events, ran for political office, and assumed positions of leadership in local organizations. In the process they became deeply involved in civic affairs, acquired respectability in business, played the role of pocket banker, and helped launch new enterprises.

Though the Jews never numbered more than three families at any one time, if the social and business columns of the local newspaper are proper indicators, their involvement in the affairs of Valdosta was inversely proportionate to their number.[16] Any movement or activity of the Jews was increasingly considered

---

[15]Telephone interview with F. S. B. Engel (New Orleans LA), 20 February 1977. During this period the Ehrlich girls were accepted into the "exclusive" Miss Simmie Coachman's School for Girls. Michael Ehrlich and Emmanual Engel served on juries, and the Jews were invited to all important social functions. See Valdosta Institute Account Book, 1876, Lowndes County Historical Society Museum, Valdosta, Georgia; Valdosta *Times*, 21 January 1907; Lowndes County, Georgia, Treasurer's Report, 100, 110, 118.

[16]For the size of the Jewish community in Valdosta and the number of Jewish businesses operating between 1866 and 1890, see *Georgia State Directory*, 1876 (Nashville TN, 1876) 324; *Georgia State Gazeteer Business Directory, 1881-1882* (Atlanta GA, 1881) 503; *Georgia State Gazeteer and Planter's Directory, 1883-1884* (Savannah GA, 1883) 853; *Georgia State Gazeteer and Planter's Directory, 1888-1889* (Atlanta GA, 1888) 669; Lowndes County, Georgia Tax Digest, 1870-1890; National Archives Record Group 58, Department of the Treasury, Records of the Internal Revenue Ser-

newsworthy, not because they were Jews, but because of their status in the community. The number and the far range of the items about them, from the important to the insignificant, reveal that they had learned how to belong; that they had succeeded in the Gentile world of Valdosta; that they and the Gentiles had found common ground; and that they had indeed become as one among them.

It would be an understatement to say they were well-liked. They had started out as pioneers of "new Valdosta," and by the 1880s they had become "living institutions" after whom the next generation of Valdostans should model themselves.[17] The Valdosta *Times* was not easily given to words of tribute, but when it came to the German Jews there was lavish praise. "We wish him unalloyed happiness," an editor wrote on the occasion of Michael Ehrlich's marriage in 1883.[18] "They will be missed," an editor mournfully wrote in 1885, when George and Lena Ehrlich retired to Savannah. "Worse people than the Ehrlichs have lived among us. The Times wishes them well wherever they may go."[19] And of Emanuel Engel, ignored in 1874, the *Times* wrote touchingly in 1888, "May his shadow never grow less."[20] Indeed, if these German Jews had remained in Valdosta, they no doubt would have been counted among the prominent families of established society. The last of them, however, Henry Ehrlich, left for Savannah in 1889.

It was not until late 1891 that the vanguard of the Russian Jews arrived in Valdosta.[21] Over the next fifteen years a loose community

---

vice, International Revenue Assessment Lists, 1865-1866, District 1, Division 9; ibid., Internal Revenue Assessment Lists, 1867-1874, District 1, Division 9; Population Schedules of the Ninth Census of the United States, 1870, National Archives microfilm no. 593, roll 163; Population Schedules of the Tenth Census of the United States, 1880, National Archives microfilm no. T-9, roll 155. Records of R. G. Dun & Co., Georgia, 34, Passim, Harvard Business School, Baker Library, Manuscript Division.

[17]Wisenbaker, "First Impressions of Valdosta in 1863," 14.

[18]Valdosta *Times*, 3 November 1883.

[19]Ibid., 27 June 1885. When George Ehrlich's wife died at Quincy, Florida, in 1885, the Valdosta *Times* published a rare full-column obituary.

[20]Ibid., 21 September 1889.

[21]Joe Marks came from Americus, Georgia, and arrived in Valdosta in mid-1891. He opened a store on Hill Avenue and first advertised in the 27 June 1891 issue of

of about thirteen ever-changing families formed, which stabilized into a community of about nineteen families by 1920 and thirty families by 1940.[22] During this period relations between Jews and Gentiles underwent a transition. They passed from Margaret Varnedoe's intimate depiction, "one of us," to a distant impersonal characterization, "our Hebrew colony."[23] One of the contemporary Jews placed the burden of blame for this change solely on the Jews themselves: "They had a fear of the *goyim*. It was as if they had the horns. They were still living in the shtetl."[24]

At a distance it does seem as if the ghost of the shtetl with its huddled defensive instinct continued to haunt the Russian Jews. A closer look, however, reveals a complex and diverse group of forces at work. First, the itinerant nature of the Jewish community between 1900 and 1920 meant that the majority of its members were always relative strangers in Valdosta. They never really had the time and opportunity to overcome both the suspicion that greets outsiders and the insecurity of being a stranger. Consequently, it was only natural that these Jews would feel freer and more at ease with their own kind. By their "own kind," they meant one of two things. They meant a cultural affinity of shared experiences that drew them together as a counterbalance to the self-consciousness of being different and somewhat isolated. "We all weren't related, but we were related," avowed an early member of the Lazarus family.[25] Thus their "own kind" meant family. The majority of these Jews—Myers, Blacks, Pearlmans, Steins, and Lazaruses—who settled in Valdosta were all related. The had been brought to the area

---

the Valdosta *Times* with the following statement: "Who is Marks? What is Marks? Where is Marks? Marks is the Cheap John Clothier."

[22]To identify the Jews in Valdosta a search was made of property records, state and city court records, citizenship papers, census bankruptcy records, cemetery records, voter registration, tax records, interviews, immigration records, city council minutes, business license records, school records, and marriage records.

[23]Valdosta *Daily Times,* 21 December 1908.

[24]Interview with Harry Abrahams (Valdosta GA), 5 May 1976.

[25]Interview with Mrs. Louis Garr (Raleigh NC), 10 March 1978.

from Lithuania by the patriarch, Dave Pearlman of Americus, Georgia. On Ashley Street the majority of these Jews worked, competed, and argued together. On Troup Street they lived and played together. Both streets were like pieces of their Lithuanian hometowns of Sadowa and Bessogolia in Kovno Gubernia transplanted to Valdosta, Georgia. On the weekends they socialized together. The other members of the family from nearby towns would gather at Mother Lazarus's house in what was a ritual recommitment to the family—not Valdosta—as the center of their life and activity.[26] And when Dave Pearlman arrived, "they threw out the red carpet and brought out the good dishes," testified one of the early Jews.[27] Thus the commitment to their "own kind" acted as an isolating force, making it only too easy to accept the comfortable presence and mutual support of *landsmenschen* rather than challenge the unknowns of the Gentile world.

The hesitancy of these Jews to test the Gentile waters was caused by other conditions. Only recently had they emigrated from the restrictions of both an autocratic Russian society and a formalized shtetl culture. They had not as yet had the time to assess the practical strength of American democracy and its particular application in Valdosta society. Their difficulty stemmed partly from the apparent ease with which Gentiles resorted to violence against anyone who angered or threatened them—Negro, Mormon, Catholic, Syrian, Leo Frank.[28] They were also confused by what seemed to them to be a inconsistency of Gentile attitudes. From 1902 to 1906, for example, the newspaper ran front-page editorials condemning the treatment of the Jews in Russia and endorsing all protests to the tzar. And yet, while it published eyewitness reports of

[26]Interviews with Louis Lazarus (Valdosta GA), 9 February 1975; Mrs. Nathan Zelkind (Valdosta GA), 10 February 1976; Mrs. Louis Garr (Raleigh NC), 10 March 1978; Sam Kalin (Hendersonville NC), 24 November 1976; Mrs. Joe Gottlieb (Birmingham AL), 12 December 1976; and Fannie Lazarus (Jacksonville FL), 16 April 1976.

[27]Interview with Mrs. Louis Garr (Raleigh NC), 10 March 1978.

[28]Interviews with Sam Kalin (Hendersonville NC), 24 November 1976; Mrs. Joe Goldstein (Thomasville GA), 10 January 1976; and Mrs. Natalie Rosenberg (Thomasville GA), 22 January 1976.

the Kishinev pogrom and supported eagerly Ida Marks's fund drive to aid the beleaguered Russian Jews, it also displayed a nativism that pictured the Russian Jew as Europe's unwanted flotsam.[29] In 1914 and 1915, the Jews read condemnations of the trial and lynching of Leo Frank in the local newspaper while hearing comments that he deserved what he got. As one of the Jews on the scene summed it up: "We never knew what they were thinking. I guess that's why we never trusted them."[30]

Not knowing what to expect from the Gentiles, and thinking the non-Jews did not know what to expect from them, the Jews saw their relationship with the Gentiles as a boxing match in which distance offered a safety from punishing blows: "Anti-semitism didn't exist as long as you kept your place"; "We didn't try to mingle into the Gentiles' business"; "We'd get out of the way for them"; "Never ran for political office. That was for the *goyim*." Without any blows struck, even at the height of the Leo Frank episode, the Jews tried to convince themselves that there was no bout in the first place: "We got along fine"; "Valdosta was good to the Jews"; "They left us alone."[31] Yet there always lurked in their hearts suspicions that demanded they keep up their guard: "I was always treated nice, but there was always that undercurrent," explained Esther Podem, "You couldn't get away from it. It was 'Miss' to my face, but still 'that Jew' behind my back."[32]

These Jews may have distrusted the Gentiles, and they may have been suspicious of them, but they truly wanted to belong. The means available, however, seemed unreasonable; many of them had concluded soon after their arrival that to become an American required that they become a "naturalized Christian": "You had to be a Christian to do this and to do that," exclaimed Annie Lee Garr.

---

[29]Valdosta *Daily Times*, 30 March; 20 June; 8 September; and 4 April 1905.

[30]Interview with Sam Kalin (Hendersonville NC), 24 November 1976.

[31]Ibid., 30 November 1976; Louis Lazarus (Valdosta GA), 2 March 1976; Harry Abrahams (Valdosta GA), 12 May 1976; Frank Meyers (Tallahassee FL), 9 June 1976; Sam Myers (Tallahassee FL), 11 June 1976; and Hannah Golivesky (Valdosta GA), 4 February 1977.

[32]Interview with Esther Podem (Thomasville GA), 4 January 1977.

"It was your Christian duty to join social clubs; it was Christian to belong to charity groups; Thanksgiving was a Christian holiday; July 4th was a Christian holiday. Landsakes, I was even asked how come I talked Christian instead of Jewish!"[33] Belonging, then, always seemed to be at their expense; it was always on the Gentiles' terms: "I remember some time after World War I when I came to Valdosta I was asked, 'Are you Jew or American,' as if I had to make a choice," explained Ruth Landey. "I could never understand why they couldn't believe I could be both."[34] Those who rejected the validity of such a choice and recognized their inability to change Gentile views resigned themselves to belonging to a separate colony of Jews living in America. Others, such as Esther Handelman, however, were tempted: "I didn't talk about Judaism. I was reluctant about that. I wanted to act as much like they did because I wanted to be accepted. And in order to be accepted I tried to help them forget I was Jewish. I thought once it was evil to be Jewish. I soon was ashamed. How could I forget being Jewish when they wouldn't let me?"[35] Nevertheless, others kept on trying, but such efforts were for the most part in vain.

The truth of the matter was that Jews and Gentiles had little in common socially or culturally. It was not a situation that had been deliberately created by either Gentiles' prejudice or a shtetl mentality. Rather, it was the result of forty years of Valdosta social and economic development. In the years immediately following the Civil War, the Valdostans developed an open, pioneering society that accepted any white person who could contribute to the viability and stability of both the economic and social order. As the years progressed, however, Valdosta began weaving a tightly knit social fabric whose pattern was designed by those pioneering families who were in the process of becoming the economic, social, and political leaders in the community. These families had included the German Jews, but they were no longer present. The Russian Jews had played no role in this structuring of Valdosta society. Conse-

---

[33]Interview with Mrs. Louis Garr (Raleigh NC), 10 March 1978.

[34]Telephone interview with Ruth Landey (Valdosta GA), 5 December 1975.

[35]Interview with Esther Podem (Thomasville GA), 4 January 1977.

quently, upon their arrival they found that the native Gentiles were unwilling to accept them as social equals. The simple credentials for acceptance into Gentile society that characterized the post-Civil War period had, by the turn of the century, given way to a complex combination of changing criteria, few of which the Russian Jews could meet.

Peddling was not an acceptable trade in these non-Jewish circles. Patterson Street was the only "proper" commercial street. Ashley Street, where the Jews had located their stores, was degradingly known as "Nigger Street" because on it were located the saloons and stores where blacks traded. Business clientele was another social indicator that placed the Jews close to the bottom, since they not only dealt with Negroes, but because "they even let them try on the clothing or at least touch it."[36] Hill Avenue was the only really acceptable street on which to live. All others were graded socially downward, with Troup Street at the lower end of the scale. "We sometimes called it Jew Street. We didn't mean nothing by it, but it certainly wasn't like the other streets," testified one of the Gentile matrons.[37] To live above or behind a store, as did the early Russian Jews, was an impropriety. Longevity of residence, economic status and, of course, church membership were other considerations that almost automatically excluded the Jews from the various Gentile circles.[38] Little wonder the Jews did not mingle with any Gentiles beyond the immediacy of their neighborhood. Such mingling, however, seems to have been limited to an occasional over-the-fence conversation or a baked cake. "Generally our relations with the *goyim*," observed one of the founding Jews, "ended at closing."[39]

As far as Gentile society was concerned, the Jews just did not fit in. "They were merely peddlers at heart: friendly, but rough-edged, not worthy to be taken to your bosom."[40] Such was the tes-

---

[36]Interview with Mrs. George Sherman (Valdosta GA), 10 November 1975.

[37]Interview with Regina Demming (Valdosta GA), 5 November 1975.

[38]Interview with Ruth McMillan (Valdosta GA), 15 December 1975.

[39]Interview with Sam Kalin (Hendersonville NC), 24 November 1976.

[40]Interview with Regina Demming (Valdosta GA), 5 November 1975.

timony of one of the leaders of Valdosta's Gentile society. If there were any questions whether this view was an accurate assessment of the Russian Jews, there was sufficient publicity of arguments and fights among the Jews, not to mention newspaper stories of rabbis of visibly questionable character, to assure those Gentiles who wished to be convinced that the Jewish "colony" indeed lacked civility.[41]

The two-year break in the continuity of the Jewish presence in Valdosta was not particularly crucial, for had the German Jews remained in the community it is not likely they would have been willing to be the means by which the Russian Jews might have entered Gentile circles. In fact, the attitude of the Russian Jews towards those in Valdosta who they thought were German Jews and towards the few German-Jewish wives was such that the German Jews would have been unable to help their Russian coreligionists even if they were so inclined. The crucial element in this social compound was the timing of the arrival of the Russian Jews, for three steps had been taken within Gentile society that solidified its structure before the Russian Jews could establish their presence.

First, between 1890 and 1895, the basic standards for social position were laid down. Second, throughout the 1890s the majority of the churches were formally organized, around which all subsequent social activity would revolve. And finally, between 1900 and 1903, the women's clubs, civic clubs, and social clubs were organized as means of permitting Valdosta Gentiles "to exercise their Christian duty in the performance of their community and civic responsibilities."[42] These organizations became the watchtowers for Gentile society. Members guarded the exclusiveness of these organizations and displayed their affiliation as a prestigious badge of

---

[41]The 2 March 1910 issue of the Valdosta *Daily Times* headlined a story entitled, "A Rabbi Gets in Trouble." In a 21 December 1908 issue of the same paper a story entitled, "More Trouble in the Hebrew Colony," detailed a fistfight among Jews. One *shochet* was known to have pawned his knife on several occasions for pints of whiskey. The knife was returned by a Baptist minister who lived behind the Lazaruses on Troup Street. Interview with Harry Abrahams (Valdosta GA), 5 May 1976.

[42]Valdosta *Daily Times*, 13 June 1903.

social prominence. At times such social activities seemed even more important than church membership.[43]

The fabric of Gentile society, however, was not woven so tightly that under the right circumstances Jews could not enter. The experience of Joe Marks and Harry Abrahams demonstrates the existence of such opportunities. On the surface, these two Jews had little in common that would explain why they were the only two to be accepted into the higher echelons of Gentile society. Joe Marks had been in the United States twenty years, learning how to be both American and Jew, before he arrived in Valdosta in 1891. Harry Abrahams was only eighteen years old when he settled in Valdosta in 1916, after a year's stay in Savannah. Marks, though born in Lithuania, was "paraded" by his wife before the Gentiles as a German Jew. Consequently, their attitude was influenced by their recent associations with the Ehrlichs and Engels. In deference to his wife, it was an impression Joe Marks never corrected, even though it caused friction between him and the Russian Jews. On the other hand, Harry Abrahams, with his thick accent and language difficulty, could hardly hide his Polish ancestry. Marks operated a fashionable clothing store on Patterson Street and lived on Hill Avenue. Harry Abrahams had a jewelry store on Ashley Street and lived near Troup Street. A caustic comment by a fellow Jew offered an oversimplified explanation for their relationship with the Gentiles: "They were elite Jews who didn't want to be Jewish. They were thought of as traitors to their people."[44]

This judgment, however, is neither fair nor accurate. It is true that Joe Marks did not socialize with other Jews except for a weekly poker game. Even when he did mingle with Jews, it was with German Jews, the Oelsner family, from nearby Quitman. He never hesitated to go to a church to listen to a good sermon, and his son sang in church choirs. Nevertheless, Joe Marks conducted the first Jewish services held in Valdosta in 1892, and he continued to act as a lay rabbi for the Valdosta Jewish families for the next sixteen

---

[43]Ibid., 9 September 1907.

[44]Interview with Esther Podem (Thomasville GA), 4 January 1977.

years.[45] He was instrumental in the formation of the Valdosta He-brew Congregation in 1908, and offered to fund one-half the cost of purchasing a building for a synagogue. When the other Jews pre-ferred to isolate themselves, he convinced them to hold public Sab-bath services on the courthouse steps so Gentile and Jew might learn something of each other. Indeed, his economic prominence and leadership in the Jewish community earned him the title "king of the Jews."[46] Harry Abrahams, like Joe Marks, never ignored a Jew in need. Both he and his wife became leaders in the congre-gation after the construction of the temple in 1920.

The absence of restricting family ties set Marks and Abrahams apart from the other Jews in Valdosta and allowed them to be a part of the Gentile community. Moreover, though they had arrived in Valdosta at different times, each moment was a focal point in de-termining Gentile-Jewish relations. Because Joe Marks arrived just prior to the final formalization of Valdosta society and because he was mistaken as a German Jew, he was afforded the opportunity of merging with this Gentile social hierarchy that was not given to succeeding Jews. Harry Abrahams came at a time when that social structure was unraveling under the impact of the aftermath of World War I and just before the structuring of the Jewish commu-nity around the temple. Consequently, he too was offered the op-portunity of weaving himself into the new social fabric of the Gentile before it again became tightly knit.

The question arises, then, why didn't the other Jews take ad-vantage of the changes, however slight, in Gentile society after World War I? The answer lies in two areas. First, Harry Abrahams had arrived in Valdosta with a "clean slate"; that is, while the social status of the resident Jews had been firmly established in both the Gentile and Jewish minds, his was not. The second factor was the building of the temple in 1920. For the resident Jews, the temple was an extension of their "family." It became the center of Jewish social activities as the churches were for the Gentiles. The Sunday school,

---

[45]Telephone conversation with Leonard Kornman (Nashville TN), 1 February 1977.

[46]Valdosta *Daily Times*, 9 September 1902; 22 February, 6 May 1909; Louis Laz-arus (Valdosta GA), 3 March 1976.

the women's auxiliary, the Sisterhood, the Purim balls, and Cha-
nukah dances were the Jewish counterpart to the Gentile charitable
and social organizations wherein the Jews could display their moral
responsibility and reinforce their cultural identity. For the Jews who
arrived after 1920, the push of a closing Gentile society combined
with the pull of an active temple congregation proved to be sufficiently strong to overcome the inclination to become "as one of us."

Perhaps the relationship that developed during the 1920s and
1930s can best be expressed in two statements. "Why should I have
gone where I wasn't wanted," asked one of the Jewish matrons.
"Who needed them anyway? I had my temple, my family and my
heritage. I didn't come here without anything like a *schwartzer*. The
hell with them I said."[47]

"I was once asked by the aunt of a Jewish acquaintance in high
school," said one of the present-day leaders of Gentile society of her
experiences in the mid-1930s, "if I was a Jew or Gentile. Well, for
the life of me here I was fifteen years old and I had never heard the
term 'Gentile.' I knew I wasn't Jewish, so I said, 'I'm Gentile.' You
see, we never thought of such things because we never did things
with them. They were so few. We hardly knew they existed. Besides, they had their own church."[48]

[47]Interview with Mrs. Fannie Fisher (Charleston SC), 29 November 1975.

[48]Interview with Mrs. Susan McKey Thomas (Valdosta GA), 17 January 1976.

2

Moses Elias Levy and Attempts to Colonize Florida

by Joseph Gary Adler

While historians have long recognized that Mordecai M. Noah's abortive Ararat project was only one of several early proposals to establish a religiously homogeneous agricultural colony, they have passed lightly over Moses Elias Levy's related attempts to colonize Florida.[1] Given Noah's greater prominence in the American Jewish community, his relations with major figures in the Jacksonian period, and his earlier diplomatic service, this neglect is not surprising. It has also been observed that Noah, as a newspaper editor with a flair for publicity, was better situated than Levy to promote his settlement project. Noah's 1825 "Proclamation to the Jews,"

---

[1] Students of Florida history have written on Levy more than have specialists in American Jewish history. See Elfrida D. Cowen, "Moses Elias Levy's Agricultural Colony in Florida," *Proceedings of the American Jewish Historical Society* 25 (1917): 132-34; George R. Fairbanks, "Moses Elias Levy Yulee," *Florida Historical Quarterly* 19 (January 1940): 165-67; Leon Huhner, "Moses Elias Levy, Florida Pioneer," *FHQ* (April 1941): 319-45; Samuel Proctor, "Pioneer Jewish Settlement in Florida," *Proceedings of the Conference on the Writing of Regional History in the South* (Miami FL, 1956) 81-115; Jacob Toury, "M. E. Levy's Plan for a Jewish Colony in Florida—1825," in Lloyd P. Gartner, ed., *Michael: On the History of the Jews in Diaspora* (Tel Aviv, 1975) 3:23-33.

which called for the establishment of a City of Refuge, is remembered, even though the plan was quickly abandoned in the wake of public criticism within the Jewish world. In contrast, Levy's twin proposals for the establishment of a Jewish boarding school on the site of a religious agricultural community have been largely forgotten.

Yet Noah's quixotic proclamation becomes more comprehensible when seen against the background of Levy's earlier attempts at colonization. Levy, rather than Noah, seems to have been the guiding force in the efforts of a coterie of young Jewish leaders to aid their brethren overseas, while simultaneously promoting the creation of a progressive Jewish school. It will be seen that Noah endorsed Levy's school plans and even joined with others to invest in a Florida land company that had been created to help finance Levy's colonization efforts. Not until 1825, by which time Levy's plans to attract Jewish settlers to Florida had begun to falter, did Noah revive an earlier proposal for the purchase of Grand Island.

Who was this man, Moses Elias Levy, who burst upon the American scene in 1818, and immediately assumed a leadership role among young Jewish activists? Levy was born in Mogador, Morocco, on 11 July 1781.[2] His father, Elijah Levy-Yuly, following a century-long family tradition, had been "merchant of the sultan" in Mogador and Tangier, and finally vizier at the end of Muhammad's reign.[3] Following the overthrow of the sultan by his son Moulay Yazid in 1790, the new ruler carried out severe pogroms against his Jewish subjects in general, and his father's close advisers in particular. Although there are conflicting accounts of the fate of Elijah, it

[2]The following data is from the United States District Court, Philadelphia, Reports of Aliens Commencing January 5, 1816, Book B, 163: "June 8, 1821. Moses Elias Levy, born in the City of Morocco, [Mogador] in the States of Barbary 11 June 1781. Migrated from Havanna [sic], arrived Philadelphia 28 June 1818. Intends to settle in Phila." (signed ME Levy)

[3]According to David Corcos, the name Yuly is a Hebrew acrostic, which is derived from the following phrase in the Book of Psalms, 86:9: "They (all the nations) shall come and bow down before Thee." Rabbi Samuel Levy Aben-Yuly (d. after 1740) was the first family member to append this honorific appellation to the family name of Levy. See *Encyclopedia Judaica*, 17 vols. (Jerusalem, 1971) 16:894-96.

seems that he fled to England and died there in 1799.[4] His wife (who may have been British) and young children found refuge in nearby Gibraltar, and it was there that Moses Levy spent his formative years. Here he apparently received an intensive Jewish education, for his surviving letters and published writings are studded with biblical and rabbinic quotations.[5]

Following his introduction to French doctrines of materialism at the age of fifteen, Levy began to question his inherited religious beliefs. His faith was suddenly restored, however, following an incident in the synagogue in which Levy believed that his life had been spared by divine intervention. He immediately took an oath that he would never again doubt the Bible.[6] Levy gradually developed a religious philosophy that combined a love of man and providence, and an unshakable belief in the divine authority of the Bible. Adhering to the written text of the Torah, Levy proposed to dispense with all rabbinic interpretations that modified even the simplest meaning of the text. Although Levy departed from Orthodox Judaism in rejecting the Oral Law, he also denounced those who adhered to an "individual religion." Rather, Levy stressed the need for a community of believers who would share a common creed and follow a prescribed order of religious observances. He even contended that children belonged to the religious community and not to their parents, a view that contributed to his sons' later alienation from their father. By 1818 Levy had come to believe that all his efforts must be devoted to the regeneration of his people. Hence he

---

[4]Corcos maintains that Elijah Levy fled to England and died there as a Jew ca. 1799. Family tradition also affirms that England, not Egypt, was his place of refuge. Samuel Romanelli, who spent more than four years in Morocco, leaving in the spring of 1790, maintains that Elijah Levy converted to the Islamic faith in order to save his life. However, Romanelli trys to discredit Levy and others of the sultan's court; hence he must be read with caution. See J. H. Schirmann, ed., *Massa ba-Arav* (Jerusalem, 1968, Hebrew ed.) 76ff. For a description of the suffering of Moroccan Jewry during the reign of Mulay-Yazid, see H. Z. Hirschberg, *A History of the Jews in North Africa*, 2 vols. (2nd rev. ed.; Leiden, 1981) 1:293-301.

[5]"Notes of Manuscript Writings of M. E. Levy," David L. Yulee Papers, P. K. Yonge Library of Florida History, University of Florida.

[6]Moses Elias Levy to Rachel DaCosta, 1 September 1853, Yulee Papers (marked "not sent").

was prepared to contribute to this cause most of the fortune that he had acquired as a St. Thomas lumber merchant and later as a military contractor for the Spanish government in Havana.[7]

Levy's theological views were formulated in an era of religious experimentation in which laymen, rather than rabbis, took the initiative. He almost surely derived some of his innovative ideas from the writings of Israel Jacobson, a wealthy businessman from the German states and progenitor of the Reform movement in Europe and America. Levy, with his acceptance of the divine authority of the Torah, his advocacy of an enlightened religious despotism, and his disapproval of attempts to form a common Judeo-Christian religion, was much closer in outlook to Jacobson than to Moses Hart, a contemporary advocate of a universal religious system based upon Deistic principles.[8]

It was because of his opposition to such assimilationist approaches that Levy determined to found a colony for European Jews. Subscribing to the growing belief that Jews would gain increasing acceptance from their Gentile neighbors by giving up their age-old commercial pursuits for a return to the soil, Levy began to formulate plans for a religious agricultural community. While visiting London in 1816, Levy met Frederick S. Warburg of Hamburg, who was then employed as an agent for a group of Jewish and Christian families who were seeking a site in the New World suitable for vine culture.[9] Although Levy then resided in Havana, he informed Warburg of his intention of settling a number of families in America.[10]

---

[7]Levy to Samuel Myers, 18 October, 1 November 1818, Myers Family Papers 2327, Hebrew Union College, American Jewish Archives, Cincinnati, Ohio.

[8]Jacob R. Marcus, *Israel Jacobson* (Cincinnati OH, 1972) passim and "The Modern Religion of Moses Hart," in Marcus, *Studies in American Jewish History* (Cincinnati OH, 1969) 121-53.

[9]Frederick S. Warburg's family may have originated in Westphalia. He was a distant cousin of Daniel Warburg, the first member of the German-Jewish family of bankers and philanthropists to come to this country. Warburg was reported to be living in Alachua County in 1823. However, he later returned to the German states. See Bertram Korn, *Early Jews of New Orleans* (Waltham MA, 1969) 46-52.

[10]United States Congress, House, "Deposition of Frederick S. Warburg," H. Doc. 10, 27th Cong., 1st Sess., 32.

Levy's extended visit to the United States in 1818 provided him with an additional opportunity to gauge the direction of Florida's future. He also noted the contrast between the Jewish communal leadership in America and Europe. Americans such as Mordecai Noah and Rebecca Gratz, while loyal to their heritage, were also innovative and cognizant of the need to develop democratic communal institutions. The United States, with its buoyant spirit, appeared to Levy as an ideal location for a model community of believers.[11]

Among the most important of the personal relationships that Levy cultivated at this time was that with the Moses Myers family of Norfolk, Virginia. Arrangements were made for Levy's younger son, David Levy (who would later become Florida's first United States senator, and would change his surname to Yulee), to board with the Myers family while attending the prestigious Norfolk Academy. The elder Levy also won over Myers's son Samuel to his school and colonization projects, and Samuel then solicited the support of Mordecai Noah of New York and Joseph Marx of Richmond.[12] Levy was also able to persuade other young communal leaders to endorse his proposals during a visit to several Eastern seaboard communities in the winter and spring of 1821. His plan, which he outlined in a circular containing twelve resolutions, called for the creation of an educational institution for Jewish youth whose curriculum would combine Hebraic and secular studies in

---

[11]Malcolm H. Stern, "The 1820s: American Jewry Comes of Age," in Bertram W. Korn, ed., *A Bicentennial Festschrift for Jacob Rader Marcus* (New York NY, 1976) 539-49; Levy to Rachel DaCosta, 1 September 1853, Yulee Papers.

[12]Stern, "The 1820s," 541-42; Stern, "Moses Myers and the Early Jewish Community of Norfolk," *Journal of the Southern Jewish Historical Society* 1 (1958): 5-13; Levy to Myers, 18 October, 1 November 1818, Myers Family Papers, Hebrew Union College; Joseph L. Blau and Salo W. Baron, eds., *The Jews of the United States, 1790-1840*, 3 vols. (New York NY, 1963) 3:879. Levy, who had married Hannah Abendanone on St. Thomas, 16 March 1803, petitioned for a contract of divorce on 5 June 1816, which was granted by King Frederick VI of Denmark on 20 February 1818. (St. Thomas was then a Danish possession.) Levy's other son, Elias, and his daughter Rama were sent away to school, and David and Rachel left later. Their mother remained on St. Thomas alone. See communications from F. O. Bro-Jorgensen, keeper of the Danish Record Office, Copenhagen, 15 January, 8 March, and 4 July 1950, Yulee Papers.

addition to agricultural and horticultural courses. Students and faculty were to live on the site of the school, which was to consist of "a tract of land . . . in a healthy and central part of the Union." Another aspect of this plan was its provision for the education of Jewish youth of both sexes. Since the name given to this proposed school was *Chenuch* or Probationary, it was probably intended to be a secondary school rather than an institution of higher learning. Significantly, Mordecai Noah's name also appeared on this circular.[13]

Levy and the others who were interested in this project intended that several committees, each made up of four persons, would be formed in major American Jewish communities to raise funds for the school. Although a New York group, including Levy, Noah, Moses Levy Maduro Peixotto, and Judah Zuntz was established, a snag developed in the formation of other committees.[14] By July 1821 Levy had sailed for Florida, and without his leadership the project apparently became dormant.

One of the intriguing questions about Jewish colonization efforts at this time is the relationship among the plans promoted by Levy, Noah, and William Davis Robinson. Existing records shed little light on this matter, but certain inferences may be drawn from the sequence of events. Levy's colonization plan dates from at least 1816, or at least two years prior to his first known visit to the United States.[15] During this 1818 visit, Levy also discussed the purchase of public lands in Illinois with Samuel Myers and "a gentleman from Illinois," and soon thereafter Moses Myers and Israel Kursheedt of Richmond separately purchased a total of thirty-four patents of

---

[13]Circular of 9 May 1821, reprinted in Korn, ed., *Eventful Years and Experiences* (Cincinnati OH, 1954) 199-200. The other names on the circular were the Reverend Moses Levy Maduro Peixotto and Judah Zuntz, both of Congregation Shearith Israel.

[14]J. I. Cohen of Baltimore resented Levy's suggestion that Baltimore be placed under the Norfolk committee's jurisdiction. In a letter to John Myers, 24 June 1821, Cohen contended that Levy "misunderstood the native Hebrew of the U.S." Myers Family Papers, Norfolk Museum.

[15]*American State Papers*, Public Lands, vol. 3 (Washington DC, 1834) 729. In 1825 Levy recalled that he had begun to develop his "plan" as early as 1803. See Levy to Issac L. Goldsmid Esq., 25 November 1825, in Toury, "M. E. Levy's Plan," 29.

land in that territory. Levy also held a substantial interest in these public lands, but his investment was lost when Moses Myers and Sons went into bankruptcy in 1819.[16]

The object of this Midwestern land venture was to provide a central location for the aforementioned Jewish school. The establishment of the *Chenuch* was clearly of great importance to Levy, whose two sons would otherwise have had little opportunity to receive a Jewish education; he was even prepared, it seems, to sell his Florida holdings and take up residence at the school.[17] There is no indication that Noah was involved in the Illinois purchase, but he may have known of it from Samuel Myers's letter of 1819.[18]

It should be noted that 1819 was also the year that Robinson's pamphlet, which called for the establishment of a Jewish agricultural settlement "in the Upper Mississippi and Missouri territory," was first circulated in the United States. Robinson had earlier gained a certain notoriety by his ill-starred schemes for aiding South American revolutionaries, which had led to his imprisonment by Spanish authorities. It is not known what suddenly prompted this Christian merchant and propagandist to utilize his skills for a Jewish cause. Perhaps it was enmity toward Spain. More likely, Robinson's pamphlet was subsidized, if not actually commissioned, by a Jewish benefactor, for it is completely lacking in missionary content.[19]

In any event, Robinson arrived in the United States around April 1819, and promptly informed American Jewish leaders that funds for his project were available in Europe. He claimed that Lord Rothschild in England and a member of the wealthy Cardoza family on Gibraltar were prepared to finance his proposed settlement,

---

[16]Copies of correspondence between Samuel Myers, Levy, and New York agents, 19 September 1819, Myers Family Papers, Norfolk Museum; Stern, "The 1820s," 541-42.

[17]Levy to Warburg (undated), quote in U.S. Congress, House, 27th Cong. Report, 450, 59.

[18]Blau and Baron, *The Jews*, 3:885.

[19]Ibid., 879-84; Morris U. Schappes, ed., *A Documentary History of the Jews in the United States* (New York NY, 1952) 602, n. 1; Judah Zuntz to Samuel Myers, 3 January 1820, Myers Family Papers, Norfolk Museum.

with the stipulation that communal leaders in this country aid in the recruitment and settlement of the European colonists.[20] These assurances, however, were not forthcoming. Although Zuntz was not unsympathetic to this proposal, he was not able to deter Noah from pressing ahead unilaterally with his Grand Island plan. Levy was then winding up his affairs in Havana, and there is no indication that he met Robinson, whose death reportedly occurred prior to 1823.[21]

In January 1820 Noah requested authorization from the New York state legislature to purchase Grand Island as a haven for "emigrants of the Jewish religion in Europe." A bill incorporating this petition was promptly referred to a select committee, but no further action was taken.[22] Noah's plan was opposed by some legislators; moreover, state officials were not at liberty to sell Grand Island until 1822, when a boundary dispute with Great Britain over this undeveloped land was settled in favor of the state of New York. Still, Noah deferred further promotional efforts until 1824. A recent biographer attributes this hiatus to the press of other business and Noah's reluctance to proceed in the face of a cool public reaction to his plan.[23] This explanation seems incomplete, however, as Noah was to appoint himself a "Judge of Israel" in his oft-quoted address of 15 September 1825, which he immodestly described as the "Jewish Declaration of Independence."[24] This bloated rhetoric did not come from a man who would back off when confronted by public indifference to his grandiose plans.

---

[20]The person mentioned here may be Aaron N. Cardoza, a merchant who lived on Gibraltar. Cardoza's name also appears on a list of Jews contacted by Mordecai M. Noah.

[21]Zuntz described Noah as "obsessed with ambition," and noted that he had sought government patronage for his plan and an official title. Zuntz to Myers, 3 January 1820, Myers Family Papers, Norfolk Museum.

[22]G. Herbert Cone, "New Matters Relating to M. M. Noah," *Proceedings of the American Jewish Historical Society* 11 (1903):131-37.

[23]Jonathan D. Sarna, *Jacksonian Jew: The Two Worlds of Mordecai M. Noah* (New York NY, 1981) 62-65.

[24]Selig Adler and Thomas Connolly, *From Ararat to Suburbia: The History of the Jewish Community of Buffalo* (Philadelphia PA, 1960) 8.

A more likely explanation for Noah's inaction during the period 1822-1824 relates to the subject at hand. Noah may have decided to suspend, but not abandon, his own colonization efforts in order to support Levy's twin plans for a Jewish boarding school and an agricultural settlement. In addition to endorsing Levy's proposal to educate Jewish youth, Noah gave tangible support to his colonization program by purchasing shares in a Florida land company in which Levy was prominently involved.[25] For the moment, Levy appeared to have the more workable plan, for his efforts to found a Jewish colony had been taken up by the Shearith Israel group in New York City two years prior to Noah's petition to the legislature.

The circumstance that facilitated Levy's land purchases in Florida developed during the final years of Spanish rule. In 1817 the king of Spain awarded a number of large land grants to subjects who had performed services for the crown. One such grant, consisting of some part of 289,000 acres, went to the firm of Don Fernando of la Maza Arredondo and Son. It was from the Arredondo holdings, which lay in a fertile area then partially occupied by Seminole Indians, that Levy purchased some 52,000 acres in 1820—the same year that Noah first sought to acquire Grand Island. Levy made a downpayment of $25,000, and agreed to give the Arredondos an additional $10,875 when east Florida, already awarded to the United States by terms of the pending Adams-Onis Treaty, was transferred to American sovereignty after due ratification.[26]

---

[25]The following reference to Noah's holdings was found among the papers of George R. Fairbanks, the attorney who handled Levy's affairs and became a close personal friend: "That the said defendant, Mordecai M. Noah, by virtue of a certificate given by the trustees of the said Florida Association, is entitled to an undivided share or portion of the said 27,962 acres . . . equal to one thousand three hundred and sixty-five acres (1,365) thereof." Eastern District of Florida Superior Court, chancery, 1845 (in process of litigation) 11, Fairbanks Papers, Robert L. Strozier Library, Florida State University.

[26]U.S. Congress, House, Report of Mr. Burton from the Committee on Elections, Serial Set #409, 1-163; H. Doc. 27th Cong., 1st Sess., Report 10, 24-25. Levy first purchased a large tract of land on Alligator Creek, just south of Lake City. This tract was later traded to the Arredondos for a share in their grant. Levy also made other large land purchases in Florida during the early 1820s. He later estimated his total holdings at 100,000 acres, but other estimates vary from 52,000-90,000.

By assuming title to a portion of the Arredondo holdings, Levy undertook to fulfill, on a prorated basis, the firm's agreement to settle a designated number of families within three years of purchase. Levy was subsequently given a one-year extension to 1825, by which time he was supposed to have induced 200 families to settle in a remote inland area partially controlled by Indians.[27] In light of these circumstances, Levy had no choice but to open his settlement to all persons, regardless of religious creed.

Levy engaged two Floridians well known to the Seminole Indians, who were then in what is now Alachua County. Horatio S. Dexter and Edward M. Wanton were to clear a tract of land at Micanopy in preparation for the arrival of new settlers. While these agents succeeded in pacifying the Indians, their activities angered Territorial Governor Andrew Jackson and Secretary of State John C. Calhoun. Jackson described Wanton and Dexter as "profligate characters" deserving of expulsion from the peninsula or even worse. The general also denounced the recent Spanish land grants as fraudulent.[28]

Despite this official opposition, work on the Micanopy settlement proceeded. Settlement began in November 1820, and soon afterward Levy instructed Warburg to start bringing his families to Florida. However, Warburg disembarked at a Northern port, where he remained for some time, awaiting the arrival of another group from Europe. Following the appearance of this new contingent, the settlers began their long journey to Florida. Although the families arrived safely at Micanopy, Levy was disappointed to learn that Warburg's party numbered only twenty-one persons, including a number of slaves. Warburg later testified that the families "principally relied upon for settlement in Alachua" had backed out at the last moment. Some remained in Europe, while others chose to settle in less isolated portions of the free states. It is most unlikely that a single Jewish family came to Micanopy.[29]

----

[27]Cowen, "Levy's Agricultural Colony," 132-34.

[28]Andrew Jackson to John C. Calhoun, 17, 20 September 1821, in Clarence Carter, ed., *Territorial Papers of the United States, Florida*, 16 vols. (Washington DC, 1934-1949) 5:205-13.

[29]*American State Papers*, Public Lands, 3:644-45; Deposition of Frederick Warburg, 32; F. W. Buchholz, *History of Alachua County, Florida, Narrative and Biographical* (St. Augustine FL, 1929) 46-52.

Despite this inauspicious beginning, Levy continued to pour money into his venture, and he even established two more plantations on the St. Johns River, south of Lake George. Although Warburg continued to correspond with prospective settlers and the tiny colony was later augmented by the arrival of new laborers, the number of colonists still totaled fewer than fifty. Nonetheless, the settlers and slaves did manage to clear and plant 300 acres, and to cut a forty-five-mile road for wheeled carriages. Approximately thirty buildings were also erected, including a sawmill, stable, corn house, blacksmith shop, and several private dwellings. A number of crops, including sugar cane, were also cultivated.[30]

By 1824 Levy had spent over $54,000 on lands and plantations that had yielded no return. He then found himself in the awkward position of being unable to sell his lands until his titles were confirmed and his holdings surveyed. In 1825, therefore, he traveled to England and the Continent in an unsuccessful effort to obtain fresh capital and revive his lagging recruitment drive.[31] In the midst of these activities, Levy learned of Noah's 1825 "Proclamation to the Jews," which was issued the same year that the completion of the long-awaited Erie Canal greatly enhanced the economic prospects of settlers on the Niagara Frontier. Concerned lest his own colony be confused in England with Noah's Ararat, Levy took great pains to assure Sir Isaac L. Goldsmid that his Florida lands had been purchased with different motives. Whereas Levy's plans for colonization were said to rest on a theological base, Noah was depicted by Levy as a man driven by cupidity and "conspicuous of late by his folly and sacrilegious presumption."[32]

While it is unclear whether Levy had abandoned all hope of further settlement in Florida by 1828, he seems to have devoted most

---

[30]U.S. Congress, House, 27th Cong., Report 450, 74; *American State Papers*, 3:717; Deposition of Frederick S. Warburg, 32; Huhner, "Moses Elias Levy," 319-45; Proctor, "Pioneer Jewish Settlement," 92-93.

[31]Levy to Charles DaCosta, 18 September 1845; Levy to Rachel DaCosta, 1 September 1853, Yulee Papers.

[32]Sir Isaac Lyon Goldsmid was the first hereditary Jewish baronet and a leader in the Anglo-Jewish struggle for political emancipation. Sir Isaac apparently did not answer Levy's letter. Levy to Goldsmid, 25 November 1825; quoted in Toury, "M. E. Levy," 29.

of his boundless energy to other causes. In addition to engaging in public discourses in England on the theological differences between Judaism and Christianity, Levy sponsored an early protest meeting against Tsar Nicholas I's initial anti-Jewish decrees. Levy, himself a former slaveholder, also promoted a plan for the abolition of Negro slavery.[33]

After crossing the ocean six times in the period 1825-1828, Levy returned to the United States, where he lived until his death in 1854. At least one of his plantations was destroyed in 1835 at the beginning of the Second Seminole War. Ultimately, Levy recouped his land investments by selling his holdings at a good price, but this did not occur until the last years of his life.[34] Several well-known American Jews are mentioned in the extended judicial proceedings involving Levy's land titles. In addition to Noah, Abraham M. Cohen of Philadelphia and Mordecai Myers of New York are listed among the seventy individuals who purchased shares in a Florida land association founded in the early 1820s, in an apparent effort to augment Levy's diminishing supply of capital.[35] According to Levy's memorial of 14 August 1823, most of these investors were "agriculturalists from New York, New Jersey and other parts," and many were "rich and opulent citizens." Levy here contended that the majority of these land purchasers planned to settle in Florida, but this seems unlikely. It is more probable that the investors sympathized with Levy's goals and, at the same time, discerned financial possibilities through investing in lands recently added to the American domain.[36]

Rebecca Gratz, while also deeply concerned about the sufferings of her European brethren, foresaw one of the main difficulties

---

[33]Ibid., 25-33; *Letters Concerning the Present Condition of the Jews, Being a Correspondence Between Mr. Forster and Mr. Levy* (London, 1829); Thomas Thrush (late captain, Royal Navy), *Letters to the Jews With a Copy of a Speech . . . Delivered by Mr. Levy of Florida* (New York NY, 1829). The speech was published in *The World*, a London newspaper, on 28 May 1828; Huhner, "Moses Elias Levy," 335-36.

[34]Levy to Rachel DaCosta, 1 September 1853, Yulee Papers; George R. Fairbanks to A. M. DaCosta, 1 July 1901, Fairbanks Papers, folio 51 (photocopy).

[35]*American State Papers*, Public Lands, 3:723-24.

[36]Ibid., 717.

that Levy would encounter. Writing in the early 1820s, Miss Gratz noted, "Some gentlemen to the south have the same object in view as Noah . . . me thinks I would place foreigners in a more interior situation, both for their own security, and that of our borders in case of war."[37]

Yet even if Miss Gratz's sensible suggestion had been adopted, it is difficult to imagine an agricultural colony populated by European Jews in early nineteenth-century Florida. Levy, reflecting back upon the collapse of his dream, exposed the crux of the problem: "It is not easy to transform old clothes men [sic] or stock brokers into practical farmers."[38] The soundness of this insight was to be confirmed many decades later by the experiences of a far larger group of Jews from Eastern Europe.

---

[37]Rebecca Gratz to a Mrs. Hoffman, ca. 1820-1822; reprinted in Schappes, *Documentary History*, 148-50.

[38]Levy to Rachel DaCosta, 1 September 1853, Yulee Papers.

3

Penina Moise, Southern Jewish Poetess

by Solomon Breibart

In the first half of the nineteenth century, Penina Moise emerged as the first American Jewish woman to achieve any fame in the field of American literature.[1] This woman, who lived in Charleston, South Carolina, pursued a literary career at a time when it was considered unseemly for women, especially Jewish women, to do so. Although women writers were expected to con-

---

[1]The first biographical sketch of Penina Moise was written by Mrs. S. A. Dinkins (née Moise), "Penina Moise," *The American Jew's Annual, 1885-1886*. Mrs. Dinkins "wrote from her personal knowledge of her aunt" and from that of other relatives. See Harold Moise, *The Moise Family of South Carolina* (Columbia SC, 1961) 71. Other primary information is found in Lee Harby, "Penina Moise, Woman and Writer," *American Jewish Yearbook, 1905-1906*; Charlotte Adams, "A Hebrew Poet of the South," *The Critic* (28 December 1889); *Secular and Religious Works of Penina Moise, with a Brief Sketch of Her Life* (Charleston SC, 1911). The latter work was by six women " who were personally acquainted with the beloved and revered authoress, either as relatives, pupils, or children of dear friends." Other published biographical sketches are by Barnett A. Elzas in *The Library of Southern Literature* (Atlanta GA, 1909); Anita Libman Lebeson, *Pilgrim People* (New York NY, 1950); *Recall to Life, Jewish Women in American History* (New York NY, 1970); Harry Simonhoff, *Jewish Notables in America 1776-1865* (New York NY, 1956); Charles Reznikoff, *Notable American Women 1607-1950* (Cambridge MA, 1971).

cern themselves with the frivolous and the ephemeral, she frequently chose to write on themes of social importance. When Isaac Mayer Wise was seeking talent for his publication *The Israelite* in the 1850s, the only American Jewish poetess he named was Penina Moise.[2] In 1870, an editorial in the 9 December issue of the *Jewish Messenger* decried the lack of literary contributions from "our American Jewesses. . .with the exception of some effusions from a Hart, a Moise, a Heineman." Her poems were accepted in periodicals from New Orleans to Boston.[3]

Penina Moise, the sixth child of Abraham and Sarah Moise, was born in Charleston, 23 April 1797.[4] About five years earlier, her parents had come to Charleston with four sons, Cherry, Aaron, Hyam, and Benjamin, after narrowly escaping with the aid of a loyal black servant from the horrors of the slave insurrection that swept Haiti. They had left behind a very comfortable life and most of their wealth. Abraham, a native of Alsace, had migrated to the West Indies, where he had met and married Sarah, whose family was highly respected in the French colony of St. Eustatius. She, twenty-five years his junior, was a woman "of handsome personal appearance" with a "bright mind."[5]

The Moise family was fortunate to have landed in Charleston. Adherents of all religious denominations had been welcome there since earliest times. Under the South Carolina Constitution of 1790, Jews were guaranteed both the religious freedom that they had enjoyed previously by sufferance and the right to vote and hold office.[6] Here Jews "never lived in a Jewish ghetto. . .nor in a ghetto of the spirit."[7] By 1794, the Charleston Jewish community numbered

---

[2]Isaac M. Wise, "The World of My Book," translated from the German by Albert H. Friedlander, *American Jewish Archives* 7 (1954) :126.

[3]The author has identified 190 hymns and over 350 poems and other writings. All possible sources have not yet been exhausted.

[4]Moise, *The Moise Family*, 61.

[5]Dinkins, "Penina Moise," 1-2.

[6]Charles Reznikoff and Uriah Z. Engelman, *The Jews of Charleston* (Philadelphia PA, 1950) 50.

[7]Ibid., 79.

over 400 persons, worshipped in an elegant synagogue, and was "the largest, most cultured, and wealthiest Jewish community in America."[8] In this pleasant environment, the Moise family flourished. By 1800, there were five more children, two girls—Rachel and Penina, and three boys—Jacob, Abraham, and Isaac.[9] The family engaged actively in the commercial, religious, and social life of the community and was known for its hard work, devotion to Judaism, and social consciousness.[10]

When Abraham died in 1809, Penina, then only twelve years old, was required to leave school because of the family's limited finances.[11] No specific information is available on her formal education, but it is assumed that she had access to the same schools as her contemporaries. A Jewish merchant wrote in 1811, "The Jews of Charleston enjoy equal literary advantages with other members of the community. . .and the Hebrews can boast of several men of talent and learning among them."[12]

Penina continued her education by studying on her own and by reading voraciously, even by moonlight at times.[13] She was influenced and encouraged by Isaac Harby, a man of brilliant intellect—teacher, editor, critic, dramatist, a founder of the Reformed Society of Israelites—and a friend of Penina's brother, Abraham. In 1828 she wrote a poem "On the Death of My Preceptor, Isaac Harby, Esq.," in which she expressed her indebtedness:

> Light of my life! . . .
> Wert thou not he from whom my spirit caught
> Its proudest aspirations to high thought?
> Whose genial beam chased intellectual gloom,
> Whose mental radiance cherished fancy's bloom,

---

[8]Congregation Beth Elohim was formed in 1749. Barnett A. Elzas, *The Jews of South Carolina from the Earliest Times to the Present Day* (Philadelphia PA, 1905) 103.

[9]Moise, *The Moise Family*, 185.

[10]Ibid.

[11]Dinkins, "Penina Moise," 2.

[12]Elzas, *The Jews of South Carolina*, 145; from a letter by Philip Cohen, of Charleston, published in Hannah Adams, *History of the Jews* (Boston MA, 1818).

[13]Dinkins, "Penina Moise," 2.

- -

34 JEWS OF THE SOUTH

> Fired with ambitious hopes my ardent soul
> And bent its energies to truth's control?[14]

In those early years, she was close to her widowed mother. She aided the family by making fine lace and embroidery.[15] This relationship became even closer when Penina's sister and all her brothers married and established their own households. Later, when her mother became a helpless invalid, Penina was her constant companion and uncomplaining nurse until her mother's death in 1842.[16]

From an early age Penina showed a talent for writing. Her brother Jacob especially encouraged her, even paying her for weekly letters.[17] Her first known published work was the poem "France After the Banishment of Napoleon," which appeared on 31 July 1819, in a Charleston newspaper, the *Southern Patriot*. Thereafter, for almost sixty years, her poems, short stories, and essays appeared also in *Godey's Lady's Book* (Philadelphia), the *Charleston Standard*, the *Commercial Times* (New Orleans), *Heriot's Magazine* (Charleston), the *Occident and American Jewish Advocate* (Philadelphia), the *Washington Union*, the *Home Journal* (New York), the *Daily Times* (Boston); and most frequently in the *Charleston Courier*, which gave her a complimentary lifetime subscription, and posthumously in *The World* (Charleston).[18] It is not known if she received any remuneration for any of her writing for these periodicals, but it is highly doubtful that she did. She seemed to be more interested in gaining recognition than monetary compensation. In "An Old Poet's Petition to Fame," she entreated,

> Listen, oh listen, to an humble bard,
> A beggar at thy door, exalted fame,
> One who has for many years labored hard

---

[14]*Charleston Mercury*, 27 December 1828; Penina Moise, *Fancy's Sketch Book* (Charleston SC, 1833) 75.

[15]Dinkins, "Penina Moise," 2.

[16]Ibid., 2, 3.

[17]Ibid., 2.

[18]Ibid. Usually her writings are signed "M. P." Note from Mrs. Lee Loeb, a pupil of Penina, to Harold Moise, Sumter SC.

A pittance of thy bay leaves to claim.[19]

In 1833, Penina Moise published in Charleston a collection of her poems entitled *Fancy's Sketch Book*. This work, containing sixty poems, many of which had appeared earlier in Charleston newspapers, was unusual in at least two respects. First, it is considered to be the first book of poetry by an American Jewess, possibly the first by an American Jew.[20] Second, she used her full name. She did not hide behind a pseudonym, as was the custom among many women writers of the antebellum period, for many thought "ink-stained women. . .detestable."[21] Commenting upon her poems, the *Charleston Mercury* said: "They give evidence of a mind of elegant taste, of a lively fancy, and a pleasant wit, and possess considerable merit as unstudied effusions."[22] In content, they vary from the frivolous—"To a Lottery Ticket," to the sentimental—"Leila, or Love's Martyr," to the serious—"Female Patriotism in Poland."

Penina dedicated her volume to the Misses Pinckney—Maria Henrietta and Harriott—the daughters of the distinguished Charlestonian Charles Cotesworth Pinckney.[23] She said, "I only obeyed that instinct in my nature which impels me to offer tribute to VIRTUE and TALENT, whatever be the sphere or their location."[24] Maria Henrietta Pinckney has been described as "a woman of masculine intellect," and Harriott Pinckney as "distinguished for benevolence and cheerful piety."[25] These were traits that Penina admired. What other connection she may have had with the Pinckneys is open to speculation; they may have been her patrons.

In 1845, Penina was invited to contribute to *The Charleston Book, A Miscellany of Prose and Verse*, an anthology of compositions by the

---

[19]*Charleston Courier*, 19 January 1866.

[20]Tina Levitan, *The Firsts of American Jewish History* (Brooklyn NY, 1957) 90. She incorrectly states date of publication as 1835.

[21]Jay B. Hubbell, *The South in American Literature* (Durham NC, 1954) 605.

[22]*Charleston Mercury*, 12 August 1833.

[23]He was a revolutionary war officer, statesman, and diplomat.

[24]Moise, *Fancy's Sketch Book*, 1.

[25]Harriet Horry Ravenel, *Eliza Pickney* (New York NY, 1896) 320.

best of the city's writers, edited by William Gilmore Simms, the outstanding South Carolina writer of the period. She submitted a poem "Miriam," and a short story "The Convict."[26]

Like most Southern women of the genteel class, Penina seems to have led a sheltered life, empty of worldly experiences. In general, she conformed to the prevalent notion that woman's sphere was "the domestic circle, the school, the hospital, and the bed of suffering."[27] Yet she was different in that she did express herself and made known her emotions and thoughts in many delightful and fanciful verses, even though they do not rank with those of an Edgar Allan Poe, a Henry Timrod, or an Emily Dickinson. Although serious problems did concern Penina, most of her work reflects the limitations placed upon the female writer of that period. These were, to paraphrase one woman writer: to be feminine, to rhapsodize over the beauties of nature and orthodox religion, and to avoid social and moral problems.[28] Penina's poems also dealt with those personal attributes that were so evident in the writings of Sir Walter Scott, who has been regarded as the favorite author of the antebellum South: Chivalry, protection of the weak, valor in battle, loyalty and self-sacrifice, open-handed hospitality.[29]

Frequently Penina composed incidental poems about political events and leaders as well as day-to-day occurrences. Her sentiments appear to have been those of a moderate Southerner. Like most of her compatriots, she seems to have had a paternalistic attitude towards the institution of slavery. This attitude is revealed indirectly in her only known poem on the subject, which was motivated by an article she had read about a dying slave. She wrote,

> No morbid discontent his mien betrayed,
> From thirst of liberty yet unallayed.
> Was he not free to mark his moral course

---

[26]William Gilmore Simms, ed., *The Charleston Book, A Miscellany of Prose and Verse* (Charleston, 1845) 94, 363-70.

[27]From a "Toast to the Ladies" by Charles H. Moise, a nephew of Penina, quoted in *The Jewish Messenger*, 19 April 1869.

[28]Hubbell, *The South*, 606.

[29]Ibid., 188, 193.

By deed that would love and respect enforce?

Tearful was he who stood beside the dead
And laid his hand upon the patriarch's head,
While memory turned back to childhood scene
When he would on his "father's playmate" lean.[30]

In the chaotic years leading up to the Civil War, the members of the Moise family were ardent states' righters and patriotic South Carolinians. Jacob, Aaron, and Abraham were influential in the states' rights movement. The younger Moises fought with the Confederacy.[31] Penina, according to one who knew her, was a "states-right woman," although not a committed secessionist.[32] In lamenting the death of John C. Calhoun in 1850, shortly after the turmoil that resulted in the Missouri Compromise, Penina proudly evoked his part in the nullification controversy of the 1830s. At the same time, however, she pleaded for national unity:

Oh, as ye group together around his grave,
Pray to the God who Freedom's blessings gave
Now and forever to remove each bar
That discord places between star and star.[33]

When South Carolina seceded in 1860 from the Union and military units were being mustered, patriotism for the state stirred her to compose a war ditty, "Cockades of Blue." One stanza rings out,

Hurrah for the Palmetto State!
Whose patriots the "Minutes" await
    That shall summon their band
    To engage hand to hand
Any foe that dare[s] enter its gate![34]

---

[30]*Charleston Courier*, 21 March 1849.

[31]Harold Moise, *The Moise Family*, passim. Edwin Warren Moise, of Sumter, organized his own company and rose to the rank of major.

[32]Harby, "Penina Moise," 24.

[33]*Charleston Courier*, 30 April 1850.

[34]Harby, "Penina Moise," 24-25.

Yet shortly after the war began, she wrote "Dialogue Between Peace and War," in whose concluding stanza she has Peace say to War,

> I cannot, I will not, resign the sweet hope
> That soon from each hand every weapon will drop
> Which by your sanguine counsel compatriots wield,
> Who in harmony once gathered fruits from my field.[35]

As strongly as Penina Moise was influenced by her Southern environment, she was more profoundly affected by her Jewish heritage. A deeply religious woman, she was closely associated with Congregation Beth Elohim in Charleston and is buried under a simple stone in its historic Coming Street Cemetery. When the synagogue built in 1794 on Hasell Street burned in the great fire of 1838, she wrote "A Poetic Homily on the Late Calamity." Its words are reminiscent of the prophets of old:

> Denounce their deities of wood and stone,
> False gods in fabric made known;
> Tell them that, when by venal impulse stirred,
> Gold is from charity to pomp transferred,
> That precious vessel is no less profaned
> Than temple cups at tyrant's orgies drained.[36]

Two years later, when a stately new edifice had been erected to replace the old house of worship in Charleston, she wrote a poem "On Beholding the New Synagogue." Always mindful of her God and the wonders of His work, she exclaimed:

> Behold, O Mighty Architect,
> What love for Thee has wrought;
> This Fane arising from the wrecked,
> Beauty from ashes brought.
>
> How shrink the noblest works of man,
> And all his boasted powers,
> Before creation's glorious plan
> From satellite to flowers[37]

---

[35]*Charleston Courier*, 5 June 1861.

[36]Ibid., 10 May 1838; *Secular and Religious Works*, 248.

[37]*Charleston Courier*, 28 August 1840; *Secular and Religious Works*, 269.

At the dedication of the temple, one of her hymns was sung. Aware of a controversy raging within the congregation, she invoked God's blessing on the congregation and prayed:

Still, still let choral harmony
Ascend before thy throne,
While echoing seraphim reply:
The Lord our God is One.[38]

At this time Beth Elohim installed an organ for regular services, the first in a synagogue in America. Answering the call for hymns in English, Penina contributed sixty of the seventy-four *Hymns Written for the Use of Congregation Beth Elohim*. Published in Charleston in 1842, this may have been the first American-Jewish hymnal.[39] By the time the second of four editions was published in 1856, revised and enlarged, it contained 190 hymns by Penina Moise. For years many of them were used by other congregations, frequently without giving recognition to their composer.[40] Eleven of them were later included in the standard hymnal used by American-Reform- Jewish congregations.[41] These hymns rose from the depth of her being. They seek to uplift the mind; they proclaim her faith; and they express belief in God's mercy through all events in every phase of life. A Christian admirer described them as "beautiful and stately songs, reminding one in their rhythmic march of the religious verses of Cowper, Pope, and Addison and other eighteenth century poets."[42]

The introduction of the organ and other reforms led to a schism in Beth Elohim, a traumatic experience for all its members. The bitter struggle for control of the congregation and its synagogue was eventually won by the reformers after a long period of litigation.

---

[38]*Secular and Religious Works*, I.

[39]Irving H. Cohen, "Synagogue Music in the Early American Republic," *Gratz College Annual of Jewish Studies*, 20.

[40]*Secular and Religious Works*, II-III.

[41]See *Union Hymnal* (Central Conference of American Rabbis, 1932).

[42]Adams, "Hebrew Poet of the South," 327.

The traditionalists seceded and formed a new congregation, Shear-ith Israel.[43] In "Lines on the Issue of the Late Hebrew Controversy," Penina expressed distress that a rupture had occurred and was saddened by "the sound of a brother's farewell"; but she rejoiced that "the struggle was over—the victory ours."[44] Soon she was called to become superintendent of Beth Elohim's sunday school—the second Jewish sunday school in America—when the first superintendent, Sally Lopez, with whom she had taught, became affiliated with Shearith Israel. For several years Penina directed the school and wrote songs, poems, and recitations for it.[45]

It may have been for these efforts, for her hymns, or both, that Beth Elohim's board of trustees offered her free seating for life and her choice of seats. She refused with dignity, continuing to pay her seat assessment as long as she was able to go to synagogue.[46] When she became blind, she no longer attended services. On Yom Kippur, following a prearranged schedule, volunteer readers came to her home to read the service.[47] In her last poem, written near her death, she would remember them and many others who had read to her:

> Praise to my young associates who delight
> To be, as 'twere, to me a second sight,
> Through which alone I may again behold
> Flowers and gems of intellectual mold.[48]

Some of Penina Moise's best poems are those that cry out against prejudice and injustice, expecially when Jews were being victimized. Her identification with her people and their struggle for civil rights and freedom from persecution is clear. In one of her ear-

---

[43]Allan Tarshish, "The Organ Case," *American Jewish Historical Quarterly* 54:401-49.

[44]*Charleston Courier*, 20 March 1844.

[45]Dinkins, "Penina Moise," 8.

[46] Congregation Beth Elohim Minutes, 4 October, 1 November 1846; Congregation Beth Elohim Cash Books (1845-1861).

[47]*Secular and Religious Works*, VIII.

[48]"A Farewell Message to all Friends," *Secular and Religious Works*, 312-13.

liest poems, "To Persecuted Foreigners," she sounds a theme echoed by Emma Lazarus's "The New Colossus" about sixty years later; she urges them "to come to the homes and bosoms of the free":

> If thou art of that oppress-ed race
> Whose name's a proverb and whose lot's disgrace,
> Brave the Atlantic—Hope's broad anchor weigh;
> A Western Sun will gild your future day.[49]

In the early 1830s the British House of Lords refused to extend to Jews in the British Isles the same constitutional rights recently granted to dissenters and Catholics.[50] Penina expressed her outrage and astonishment in "The Rejection of the Jew Bill by the House of Lords":

> It cannot be! Britannia must explode
> That dark deformity from Freedom's code.
> It shall not be! with prescient exultation
> My joyous harp rings our Emancipation![51]

When the Jews of Damascus were subjected to enormous atrocities, she denounced the persecutions and took the nations of the world to task for their failure to interfere:

> Ye delegates of nations! could ye the suppliants scorn
> From whose inspired relics revelation was born?
> Was the jealousy of faith too strong for feelings flow
> That ye the bright prerogative of justice should forego?[52]

She was distressed when America failed to intercede with the pope to seek the release of the Jewish child Mortara, who had been abducted in Italy and raised as a Catholic; and even though it was not popular among Charlestonians—Jews and non-Jews alike—to

---

[49]*Southern Patriot*, 13 February 1820; *Secular and Religious Works*, 177.

[50]Ismar Elbogen, *A Century of Jewish Life* (Philadelphia PA, 1945) 38-39.

[51]*Charleston Courier*, 14 September 1833; *Secular and Religious Works*, 212.

[52]"On the Persecution of the Jews of Damascus," *Charleston Courier*, 29 August 1840; *Secular and Religious Works*, 270.

suggest that the American government interfere with local institutions anywhere, the poetess chided her country:

> But though unmoved their marble hearts remain,
> Spirit of Liberty! passive wilt thou stand,
> Not gently send remonstrance o'er the main
> Against the wrongs by the oppressor planned?

Continuing, she bemoaned the fact that the classical heritage of Greece had more influence than the songs of David and the Ten Commandments, which were "in the language of the Hebrews given."[53]

Penina's attachment to Palestine was strong. Touched by the gift of a Rose of Jericho brought to her from the Middle East, she wrote:

> Thrice welcome, then, that withered flower from consecrated earth
> Which rightly, pious friend, you guessed for me had greater worth.

She saw Palestine as waiting patiently for the inevitable day

> When choral acclamation from the chosen of the Lord
> Shall announce that to thy borders captive Judah is restored;
> And Messiah, in the greatest of the Tabernacles, holds
> Harvest holidays to celebrate the ingathering of souls.[54]

Penina's solicitude was not limited to her people and their problems. She was highly sensitive to the needs of all people. She wrote with sadness of Greece writhing like "a living Laocoon" in the grasp of "the Turkish serpent."[55] She was moved by the tragic plight of the Irish during the famine of the 1840s and called upon "the heart and lute of every bard. . .[to] harmonize to hush Hibernia's cry."[56] In numerous poems she sought comfort for the widow, the orphan, the afflicted, and the bereaved. During the yellow fever epidemic in 1854, although she was already having diffi-

---

[53]"Mortara," *Charleston Courier*, 16 December 1858.

[54]*Charleston Courier*, 29 January 1856.

[55] Moise, *Fancy's Sketch Book*, 5.

[56]*Charleston Courier*, 24 February 1847; *Secular and Religious Works*, 188-89.

culty with her vision, she devoted long hours to nursing its victims and entertaining the convalescents with her poems and stories.[57] She was readily available to console those who were in sorrow and to rejoice with them on happy occasions. Her friends of all creeds, particularly the young, shared with her the joys of secret love affairs, engagements, marriages, and births, and sought her blessing.[58]

The poetess had become almost totally blind during the Civil War years. This condition, aggravated by neuralgia and insomnia, was a handicap that limited her physical movements, but not her active mind. Returning to Charleston after the war—she had moved to Sumter, South Carolina, in 1861 when her native city came under bombardment by Federal troops—quite impoverished, Penina joined with her sister Rachel and Rachel's daughter, Jacqueline, to open a private school in a small house provided them by her brother, Abraham. From her vast reservoir of knowledge, accumulated by years of extensive reading and intense observation, she provided oral instruction. She made the figures of literature come alive for her pupils.[59] Respected for her learning, understanding, and wit, she "created a literary salon to which the best minds of Charleston flocked. Her Friday afternoons were a center of intellectual discourse."[60] And with the aid of Jacqueline as an amanuensis, she continued to write verse almost to the end of her life.

Penina Moise died in 1880 in her eighty-fourth year. She was, in the words of Charlotte Adams, "a Jewish poetess whose life most admirably illustrates the literary idea of the Old South in the person of intellectual, talented, and alas! sadly limited womanhood; [a woman] who for many years was the literary pivot of Hebrew Charleston, and whose influence extended far beyond the circle of her co-religionists."[61]

---

[57]Dinkins, "Penina Moise," 5.

[58]Ibid., 9; *Secular and Religious Works*, VI.

[59]Dinkins, "Penina Moise," 8.

[60] Adams, "Hebrew Poet of the South," 327.

[61] Ibid.

4

Rabbi Bernard C. Ehrenreich:
A Northern Progressive Goes South

by Harold S. Wechsler

This article interprets a life, but lives are never easy to interpret. Summing up a man's life in a word like *progressive* unavoidably does an injustice. It is not simply that other roles are neglected: our subject was a loving husband and father, a committed Jew, clergyman, Zionist, a devotee to youth and to all of life. Rather, characterizations may often become substitutes for essences, and our subject's expressed values reveal a rich essence. Yet Rabbi Bernard Calonimus Ehrenreich of Montgomery, Alabama, *was* a progressive. Here we will explore his progressive commitment.

Major post-World War II accounts of American progressivism give scant attention to the presence of the Jewish clergy in the movement, yet many played rather significant roles in advancing progressive ideals. Protestant clergy often fare little better. Robert Wiebe's *The Search for Order* dismisses their role as, at best, peripheral:

> Although they finally established an organization of their own, the Federal Council of Churches, they remained institutionally weak. The major Protestant denominations had limped into a new century with a strong bias against controversy. Consequently, reform-

minded clergymen either functioned nondenominationally . . . or acted as independent spokesmen for reform. . . . They also were worried about the Protestant retreat before materialism, and usually they responded with vague doctrines that perpetuated the late-nineteenth-century vision of a general Christian unity. . . . In a sense, reforming clergymen served as the honorary chairmen of progressivism.[1]

Wiebe does not mention the role of Jewish clergy, yet Rabbi Ehrenreich's career, along with those of many colleagues, indicates that the Jewish clergy played an activist, progressive role, without a necessary recourse to nondenominationalism.

Richard Hofstadter, in his *The Age of Reform*, did recognize Protestant clergy as leaders of reform. They serve as quintessential examples of his status revolution hypothesis. Protestant clergy, Hofstadter maintained, experienced humiliation and loss of moral and intellectual deference in a rapidly secularizing society that paid increased obeisance to a gospel of wealth. "Not only were the clergy less regarded as molders of opinion, but they were expected to carry on the arduous work of their pastorates with means that were increasingly inadequate and to defer meekly to far more affluent vestrymen."[2] Such a status loss engendered an ability to identify with other disinherited groups, such as immigrants and workers. Certainly the classic confrontation between Rabbi Stephen S. Wise and Louis Marshall over control of the Emanu-El pulpit, and Wise's strong identification with progressive causes, would have proved fit grist for Hofstadter's mill, although I believe the analogy would have ultimately failed. Yet Hofstadter refrained.

What makes Hofstadter's negligence more curious is that he derived the idea of status politics from an examination of Jewish political behavior in the twentieth century. Jews have generally favored "left" solutions from 1900 on. During the Progressive period itself, roughly 1900-1914, they favored Theodore Roosevelt and Woodrow Wilson. Jewish support for liberals in the 1920s remained steadfast. By 1944, almost ninety percent of Jewish voters sided

---

[1]Robert Wiebe, *The Search for Order* (New York NY, 1967) 207-208.

[2]Richard Hofstadter, *The Age of Reform* (New York NY, 1955) 151.

with Franklin Roosevelt. The pattern continued after World War II with disproportionate support for every Democratic candidate and for alternatives from further left. Hofstadter hypothesized that Jews throughout the century experienced economic success without commensurate increases in social status and that they adhered to political positions held by their social, not economic, peers. Once he had discovered this pattern, Hofstadter was free to offer his main hypothesis: that many, if not most, Progressive leaders experienced a gap or lag between economic and social status.

One may subject this Hofstadter argument to a quick litmus test by examining the early biography of Rabbi Ehrenreich. Born on 11 June 1876, at Kis Szeben, Hungary, the son of Henry R. and Hanna Ehrenreich, Bernard arrived in America at the age of three. His father, who appears to have been an Orthodox man, migrated to America in his thirties, probably for economic reasons. Henry Ehrenreich worked as a bookbinder for most of his adult life. The family also consisted of a daughter Sarah and a second son Herman.

Bernard Ehrenreich's career as a rabbi accorded him increased amounts of status—the opposite of Hofstadter's description of Protestant clergy. One might well agree with Hofstadter about the clergy's meager means. Ehrenreich curtailed his own educational aspirations for financial reasons. He could rarely afford to attend meetings and conferences of groups in which he had commitments, and he often gave up even small material comforts because of their expense. At the same time, he helped finance his younger brother's education. While Rabbi Ehrenreich found enough satisfaction in his Montgomery pulpit to remain there almost fifteen years (he originally thought he would perhaps stay four or five years), other offers had to be taken seriously because of the economic problems he faced. And, in common with others on fixed incomes, the gradual inflation that pervaded the years prior to World War I affected Rabbi Ehrenreich's purchasing power.

On the other hand, Rabbi Ehrenreich was recognized in Montgomery as a civic as well as spiritual leader. His service as vice-chairman of the Montgomery Chamber of Commerce reflects this, as does his appointment by Alabama Governor Emmet O'Neal to serve as official representative to a convocation protesting Roumanian anti-Semitism.[3] The city's leading newspaper characterized Rabbi Ehrenreich as one of Montgomery's leading citizens.[4] The general flaw in Hofstadter's argument is that the social history of a profession may not reflect the personal histories of its practitioners. The specific flaw is that a careful analysis of the Jewish clergy and progressivism would very well have yielded a different portrait of the minister's role. Marshall Sklare and others have long argued that Jewish progressivism stemmed not so much from socioeconomic considerations as from religious impulses.[5] "Every Israelite is responsible for his fellow Israelite is the dictum of the Talmud," wrote Rabbi Ehrenreich in an early sermon. "There still remains for us the duty of helping those less fortunate than ourselves. We must strive for the attainment not in part but in whole of the principles so dear to us all."[6] Thus, whereas the Social Gospel was extrinsic to mainline Protestant thought, and only emerged at a time when that ministry experienced serious status anxieties, altruism had deep roots within Jewish tradition—roots that sprouted strong plants in fertile American soil.

Of course, various reconciliations between the Hofstadter and Sklare approaches are possible. Rabbi Ehrenreich and his colleagues were fully aware that today's altruistic gesture might very well yield tomorrow's ally. Yet such theories go only so far in the quest for essence. To make further progress one must examine progressivism from another perspective, perhaps the perspective that caused the greatest concern and debate within the movement.

With the urbanization, industrialization, and, Wiebe would add, bureaucratization in America, many realized that the resultant need for collective action seriously jeopardized individual initiative and responsiblity. Where in a society witnessing the rise of

---

[3]Emmett O'Neal to Bernard C. Ehrenreich, 20 September 1913, in Rosemary Krensky, compiler, "Gan Hadorot—Garden of the Generations, A Documentary and Pictorial History of the Waterman-Bock-Ehrenreich Family," 3, Bernard C. Ehrenreich Papers, American Jewish Historical Society, Waltham MA.

[4]Undated article in *Montgomery Advertiser*, Krensky, "Gan Hadorot."

[5]Marshall Sklare, *The Jewish Community in America* (New York NY, 1974) 285.

[6]"B'nai B'rith Day in Atlantic City" in *Jewish Chautauqua Assembly Record*, 24 July 1900, 7.

Big Business, Big Labor, and Big Government did the individual fit? Progressives themselves undertook an incredible array of collective activities, yet concern grew for the individual in a world increasingly dependent on abstract relationships.[7] This is the dilemma that confronted Rabbi Ehrenreich. In his early adult years, he gained a reputation as an organizer, and that talent served him in good stead for the rest of his life. Yet as the years passed, Ehrenreich gradually concluded that his real mission did not consist primarily of collective action but in maintaining the dignity and sanctity of the individual through personal acts. His move to Montgomery in 1906 may serve as a symbol of this shift in attitude.

"Rabbi Ehrenreich's organizing power and ability are exceptional," commented the *Jewish Ledger* shortly after World War I when it profiled the Montgomery clergyman in its "Distinguished Jews of America" column.[8] He exhibited his skill in several ways while still a student. Educated in the New York City public schools, Ehrenreich received a bachelor's degree at New York University and a rabbinical degree from the recently founded Jewish Theological Seminary. Although the fervor of the Jewish community in New York did not always pervade the seminary classrooms (Mordecai Kaplan, a seminary classmate, recalled "the wearisome days in class when [Rabbi Bernard Drachman] would begin dictating from Jewish history, preferably Graetz, and many of us would find ourselves gradually falling asleep"), the young Ehrenreich found time to be in on the founding of several of the most influential Jewish organizations of his time.[9]

Named the first recording secretary of the Federation of American Zionists, he helped launch the major Jewish political movement of the twentieth century. In addition, Zionism enabled Ehrenreich and his Jewish-American colleagues "to provide a community of interest between them and the recent Jewish immigrants [who soon composed the movement's rank and file], with whom

---

[7]Samuel Hays, *The Response to Industrialism* (Chicago IL, 1957), ch. 4.

[8]Undated article, Krensky, "Gan Hadorot."

[9]Mordecai Kaplan to Bernard C. Ehrenreich, 4 September 1945, 13 September 1945, Mordecai Kaplan File, Ehrenreich Papers.

they could share the love of Jewish culture, Jewish history, and the idea of a Jewish state."[10] If the ultimate goal of Zion's reestablishment appeared remote, at least, Ehrenreich believed, the Zionist movement could serve to welcome and acculturate the large numbers of East European Jews that were moving into the major Eastcoast cities. His reconciliation of Zionism and Americanism was employed by many others during the movement's early years. "I am an ardent Zionist," he wrote. "Assimilation with the manners and customs of the people among whom we live is highly necessary and most important, but the only trouble is that outside the United States and England, it seems that the nations of the world are unwilling to permit any such assimilation, as much as the Jews of these countries may desire it." Ehrenreich asserted the reasonableness of emigration from inhospitable countries but commented, "This does not mean that the Jew who lives in a land of freedom shall leave the same and travel to shores unknown to him."[11]

Ehrenrich adhered to these facets of Zionism throughout his long career. In 1910, he called for the abrogation of America's 1832 treaty with czarist Russia when the latter government refused to grant routine visas to American Jews.[12] Asserting the primacy of the Jew's American identity, Ehrenreich wrote, "First and foremost let it be distinctly understood that the question is not a Jewish question but an American question in which the Jewish citizen is involved. It is fitting that a government such as ours should stand for its rights and the rights of its citizens under all conditions."[13] In 1918 Louis Lipsky, then chairman of the Federation of American Zionists' executive committee, thanked both Rabbi Ehrenreich and his wife Irma for their many Zionist services.[14] The commitment of the

---

[10]Jonathan Shapiro, *Leadership of the American Zionist Organization 1897-1930* (Urbana, Chicago, and London, 1971) 33.

[11]Remarks of Bernard C. Ehrenreich in *Philadelphia Press*, 31 August 1903.

[12]For description of this controversy, see Max M. Laserson, *The America Impact on Russia, 1784-1917* (New York NY, 1962) 431-54.

[13]Undated article in *Montgomery Advertiser*, Krensky, "Gan Hadorot."

[14]Louis Lipsky to Mrs. Bernard C. Ehrenreich, 22 December 1918, Krensky, "Gan Hadorot."

Ehrenreichs never waned, and both could take pride in their own accomplishments when the state of Israel was established at the time of the Federation of American Zionist's fiftieth anniversary.

During Ehrenreich's seminary years, he grew to admire a young Columbia University Semitics professor, Richard J. H. Gottheil, an ardent Zionist and founder of the Federation of American Zionists. With Gottheil's encouragement, Ehrenreich and a fellow student set about establishing the first American Jewish collegiate fraternity. Years later, Ehrenreich would reminisce,

> One evening as we were sitting together and dreaming of the future, the thought occurred that it would be a fine idea to band together the acceptable Jewish students into a fraternity. There weren't anywhere near as many Jewish students in those days at the colleges as there are now. All of us were sober and serious-minded. I took the matter under advisement and talked it over with several others who felt the thought a capital one. We went over all the pros and cons and then decided we would organize the first Jewish college fraternity of the country.

The closeness of several New York collegiate-level institutions and the small number of acceptable Jewish students dictated the establishment of an intercollegiate body, which they named Zeta Beta Tau (ZBT).

Students from the entire city would meet at the Cafe Logeling on Fifty-Seventh Street, not to haze initiates, but to listen to speakers of the caliber of Gustav or Richard Gottheil, Stephen Wise, or Rabbi Henry Pereira Mendes. The discourses always concerned Jewish life or theology; quite often, they referred to the nascent Zionist movement. In announcing the fraternity's establishment in 1899, the *Shofar* quoted the founders as believing, "There is scarcely any college in which true democracy exists. The Gentile students in our large colleges feel and express an inexplicable aversion to our Jewish classmates." Rather than seeing themselves as retreating before Christian anti-Semitism, the ZBT founders expected that interfraternity contact would lead to closer bonds between Gentile and Jewish students. In addition, Zionism proved a major component to its mission. "The secondary objective of the fraternity is to promote Zionism and spread a better knowledge of Jewish history not alone among college men but also among the masses of people."[15]

When Rabbi Ehrenreich moved to Montgomery in 1906, he soon attempted to establish a chapter of ZBT at the University of Alabama. His first efforts proved unsuccessful, perhaps because of the small number of available students and perhaps because of the fraternity's Zionist orientation. Not long after, however, Rabbi Ehrenreich's persistence bore fruit, with the organization of the fraternity's Psi chapter at that university.[16]

When Henry Hurwitz's Menorah movement took hold among Jewish undergraduates, Rabbi Ehrenreich took immediate interest ("I look for the Menorah to grow into the most powerful influence in American Judaism," he wrote Hurwitz in 1916).[17] A nonpartisan organization aimed at the advancement and dissemination of Jewish learning founded at Harvard in 1906, Menorah grew rapidly during its first decade. Rabbi Ehrenreich took the idea one step further. Providing a pioneering example of Jewish adult education, he founded with Hurwitz's sanction a graduate Menorah society for alumni of the University of Alabama residing in Montgomery. "I look forward to receiving a copy of your program," wrote Hurwitz. "The more since you are practically plowing virgin soil so far as graduate organizations are concerned. There will be more and more call on the part of graduates all over the country for concrete plans of activities."[18] There is no doubt that Rabbi Ehrenreich was a "joiner" in the progressive tradition. He held significant positions in the Masons, the International Order of B'nai B'rith, and the Jewish Chautauqua. He described the latter as "one of the noblest undertakings of the Jew in America: the propagation of learning, the

---

[15]*The Shofar*, 14 July 1899.

[16]Bernard C. Ehrenreich, "Reminiscences of the First Generation," *Zeta Beta Tau Quarterly* 10 (December 1925) 21-23.

[17]Bernard C. Ehrenreich to Henry Hurwitz, 15 November 1916, Menorah File, Ehrenreich Papers.

[18]Henry Hurwitz to Bernard C. Ehrenreich, 3 December 1915, Menorah File, Ehrenreich Papers.

spreading broadcast of a knowledge of our beloved faith."[19] In Montogomery he served on the executive committee of the Associated Charities and was known as its "moving spirit."

Had Ehrenreich remained in New York after his graduation from the Jewish Theological Seminary, he most certainly would have attained national leadership positions in at least several groups. Instead he migrated South. In 1900 Ehrenreich received and accepted a call to Beth Israel Congregation in Atlantic City. Although he performed his duties with care, the city's status as a summer resort left him little to do for the remainder of the year. But his restlessness did not last long. Several members of Philadelphia's Adath Jeshurun chanced to attend his service one weekend, and knowing that their own rabbi had resigned, recommended that Ehrenreich receive a call. The recommendation was met with enthusiasm, first in the congregation and then among all of Philadelphia Jewry. The new rabbinical appointment, stated an editorial in the *Philadelphia Jewish Exponent*, brought to Philadelphia "a man almost at the outstart of his ministerial career who was for many years connected with the Jewish Theological Seminary. That institution is already and well represented in this city, and it is to be hoped that Rabbi Ehrenreich will add to the good work they have established for themselves and the institution to which they owe their training. Reverend Ehrenreich will have an opportunity of showing of what mettle he is made."[20]

The Philadelphia years opened some new doors while closing old ones. While espousing an essentially Conservative outlook ("Unrestricted liberalism produces the same effect as too much literalism"), he constantly gained in breadth, and several years later did not find it intellectually or emotionally difficult to accept the call of a Reform congregation. He aspired to further education. "I have decided to become a student again," he wrote soon after his arrival in Philadelphia. Undoubtedly influenced by Professor Gottheil's example, he matriculated in Semitics at nearby University of Penn-

---

[19]*Jewish Chautauqua Assembly Record*, 17 July 1900.

[20]*Philadelphia Jewish Exponent*, 12 April 1901.

sylvania. "It will be real hard work for I dare not neglect my congregational work," he wrote.[21]

The pace of this double, almost triple, existence at first exhilarated Ehrenreich. "I got back to Philadelphia [after a hectic week in New York] at 1:20 last Thursday afternoon," he related, "and after taking a cup of coffee at the Broad St. Station I made off for the university where I spent a most delightful afternoon. After supper I had resolved to remain awake until about 10 P.M., and then retire, although I was booked to address a Zionist mass meeting in the lower section of the city." Although not intending to go, the tired rabbi relented when an imploring delegation called for him. When he returned home at 12:30 A.M., he "had that awful feeling I was almost ready to drop from sheer exhaustion, still the best had to be made of the worst. I awoke Friday early and began working on my sermons, which I completed Friday at 5 P.M. They went off far better than I thought they would and all is well again."[22]

But exhaustion soon overtook exhilaration, and cutbacks had to be made. "I am enjoying my University work immensely," he wrote, "although I find that I must neglect my Talmudic work."[23] A heavy schedule forced him to give up a contemplated trip to Europe to study in a yeshivah. Soon the press of work and financial considerations (he was at this time supporting his younger brother Herman through school) led him to abandon his university studies. His marriage on 11 December 1902, to Irma Bock provided him with more responsibilities. A granddaughter of Sigmund Waterman, one of the founders of the Independent Order of B'nai B'rith, Irma graduated as valedictorian from the New York Normal College, now Hunter College. Equally at home in secular and sectarian teaching situations, she met Ehrenreich while teaching Sunday school. Upon learning the news of the impending nuptuals, Stephen Wise, who had also married into the Waterman family, congratulated his "two Sunday School teachers who at least learnt

---

[21]Bernard C. Ehrenreich to Gertude Bock, 30 September 1901, in Bernard C. Ehrenreich Memorial Book, in possession of Rosemary Krensky, Chicago IL.

[22]Idem, 10 October 1901, Krensky, "Gan Hadorot."

[23]Krensky, "Gan Hadorot."

something from each other if their pupils learnt nothing."[24] He also pointed out that the Watermans would now have three rabbis in the family. David Davidson, Ehrenreich's predecessor in Montgomery, had married the daughter of Sigmund Waterman's sister. Irma proved able to keep up with her husband's pace. Active in many Jewish causes, she became involved in such progressive activities as women's suffrage and educational reform. In one notable victory, she convinced the Montgomery school authorities to improve the sanitation of the Sayre Street School.[25] She proved a tireless worker for the reform of juvenile justice systems after becoming involved in their workings while in Philadelphia.

The arrival of Irma and Bernard's two children, Rosemary and Louis, prompted serious consideration of the family's future. Thus, when in 1906 the Kahl Montgomery Congregation called the young rabbi to its pulpit, the attractive and concrete offer brought matters to a head. Rabbi Ehrenreich was asked to follow his cousin by marriage, David Davidson, in the Montgomery pulpit. Certainly family ties helped in having his name placed before the congregation, but it was Ehrenreich's presence in the pulpit, his charisma, that led the congregation to make the actual call. Ehrenreich had achieved considerable popularity in Philadelphia. The *Philadelphia Jewish Exponent* summarized local sentiment when it characterized him as active, energetic, and capable, "and as having done good and faithful service in this city during the past five years."[26] Kahl Montgomery soon found this judgment of Ehrenreich confirmed. "The last couple of months," wrote his wife, "services on Friday evening look like a holiday service. The Temple is so crowded! An unprecedented occurrence in Montgomery."[27]

The Montgomery offer provided a degree of financial security and a considerable amount of status. But, given Montgomery's re-

---

[24]Stephen Wise to Irma Bock, undated, Krensky, "Gan Hadorot."

[25]Irma Ehrenreich to her sister, 18 December 1912, Krensky, comp., "Irma B. Ehrenreich, Collected Correspondence."

[26]*Jewish Exponent*, 1 June 1906.

[27]Irma Ehrenreich to "Baby Sister," 20 March 1910, Krensky, "Irma B. Ehrenreich Collected Correspondence."

moteness from the urban centers of the Northeast with their large
Jewish contingents, Ehrenreich knew that inevitably there would
be a cost: diminished affiliations with the many Jewish organizations he had sponsored. Security and status alone would not have
sufficed to lure him so far from family and friends. The move was
prompted by two other factors deeply rooted in Progressivism.
First there was the challenge of trying out his ideas and abilities in
a new region. "I wish I had the means to become a Jewish missionary," Ehrenreich wrote, "for I have the missionary enthusiasm."[28]
During the ensuing years, he made many friends for Zionism and
the other causes he had earlier espoused. In addition, the move
South permitted Rabbi Ehrenreich to develop in another way, that
is, to express his concern for the individual in an increasingly col-
lectivist and materialist world.

The transition from creator to disseminator did not prove difficult nor did it take very long. Shortly after his arrival in Montgomery, Rabbi Ehrenreich preached a sermon calling for the
establishment of a juvenile court. "Judaism is not alone a religion
of creed," he told his congregation, "it is a religion of action. To labor for the welfare of the government under which he lives is an in-
separable part of the religious duty of every Jew." Despite his
relatively recent arrival at Kahl Montgomery, he had already gained
a reputation for "earnestness and deep interest in humanitarian
work."[29] His interest and concern for the welfare of Southern blacks
was genuine but made his congregants apprehensive. Ehrenreich
expressed outrage when he learned that George Washington
Carver had been forced to use the freight elevator of the Exchange
Hotel in Montgomery in order to make a presentation to the United
Peanut Association's convention.[30] He made a forceful speech in
support of black higher education to a conference at Tuskeegee In-

---

[28]Bernard C. Ehrenreich to Henry Hurwitz, 5 February 1912, Ehrenreich
Papers.

[29]*Montgomery Advertiser*, 18 November 1906.

[30]Rackham Holt, *George Washington Carver—An American Biography* (Garden City
NY, 1943) 252-53.

stitute also attended by Seth Low, former president of Columbia University, and by Julius Rosenwald, the philanthropist.[31]

Sensing that black and Jewish acceptance in America was inextricably tied, Rabbi Ehrenreich's defense of black rights contained elements of both altruism and self-interest. He just as quickly censured injustice against Jews. Thus, when University of Alabama President Lincoln Hully delivered an address in Montgomery that contained some vulgar jokes concerning Jews, Rabbi Ehrenreich immediately denounced him. "Even jocularly to insult an entire people by branding them as incendiaries," he stated, "thus making them criminals of the worst type, is undignified, false and unworthy of an educator who is president of a university in the south."[32]

Nor did Ehrenreich relax his Zionist commitments. The 1917 Alabama election to the American Jewish Congress became a battle between pro- and anti-Zionists, with Rabbi Ehrenreich the leading Zionist candidate. The Zionists were well organized, so much so that opponents charged them "with working the 'steam roller'. "[33] To avoid unnecessary strife among Alabama Jews, Ehrenreich agreed to accept a compromise delegation consisting of representatives of both camps. "We conceded a great deal," Ehrenreich wrote a Birmingham associate," and my people are not particularly well pleased that we agreed to a compromise and they feel that we should have fought to the end." But, he concluded, "I am personally satisfied that we have avoided a great deal of unpleasantness which in the end would be on the credit side of our accounts."[34] "If this campaign has produced nothing else," replied his comrade, "it should be an indication to you that you have a great many friends in Birmingham who will 'go their length' for you, and from my knowledge of you, I am certain that this will be a great satisfaction

---

[31]Irma Ehrenreich to her sisters, undated (ca. 1914-1915), Krensky, "Irma B. Ehrenreich Collected Correspondence."

[32]*The Jewish American*, 1 May 1908.

[33]D. Abelson to Bernard C. Ehrenreich, 14 May 1917, AJC election, 1917 File, Ehrenreich Papers.

[34]Bernard C. Ehrenreich to Isaac Abelson, 12 June 1917, ibid.

to you."[35] Ehrenreich's election to the congress was by a large margin, and he served with distinction.

The historian is confronted with a dilemma when he attempts to document someone's concern for the individual. Many such actions never become recorded; organizational affiliations produce archival materials while individual mitzvoth rarely do. Yet in Rabbi Ehrenreich's case, the historian can rely on a rather unique set of materials: correspondence between him and young American soldiers stationed near Montgomery at Camp Sheridan during World War I. The rabbi's presence elicited intimate and searching response from all those with whom he came in contact. This proved especially true for Jewish soldiers, many away from home for the first time and most on their way to the European lines. Ehrenreich did not serve as an army chaplain, partly because such service entailed an unaffordable loss in salary, and partly because he believed that his welfare work exceeded in importance that which he could accomplish as a chaplain.[36] "As an officer I have my limitations, as a welfare worker I have none," he told Cyrus Adler.[37]

Rabbi Ehrenreich demonstrated his concern in many ways. He regularly taught an English class at the camp for over 150 illiterate soldiers. Sunday night was open house at the Ehrenreichs': "They come to my home between 3:00 and 9:00 P.M., anywhere from forty to fifty boys," he wrote. "Those who happen to remain here between the hours of 5:30 and 6:30 are here for supper and I have around my table for Sunday night supper as many as twenty-five."

---

[35]Isaac Abelson to Bernard C. Ehrenreich, undated (June 1917) ibid.

[36]He wrote Cyrus Adler in 1918: "Were it possible for me to live on the income of a first lieutenancy, I would without hesitation enlist in the service. The pay of a first lieutenant is about $166. a month. As officers live and dress I should be obliged to spend at least half of that on my own person and it would not be possible for my family to live on the other half. From that standpoint I cannot in any way consider the matter. If there were not men in the country who had no dependents, I should at once consider the matter regardless of the financial side. But there are any number of Rabbis who besides being independent of wives have incomes of their own, and others again who have wives but no children, and good incomes other than their salaries. I think that these men ought to be drafted into the service if not by our country by the Rabbinate itself." See Bernard C. Ehrenreich to Cyrus Adler, 3 October 1918, Cyrus Adler File, Ehrenreich Papers.

[37]Ibid.

After dinner came discussions. Once, he reported, "We had with us a Jewish boy from Cincinnati, Dan Segal by name. He had been sent by the government as an orderly for Major General Treat on the expedition to France. Dan Segal had been two weeks in the trenches so I had him describe his experiences and impressions while there."[38]

The variety of selfless acts Ehrenreich undertook constantly expanded. He interceded with a soldier's family to get his bad debts paid off.[39] He secured the discharge of a soldier.[40] He allayed parents' fears that their son, who suffered from rheumatism, would be sent overseas.[41] He comforted a mother upon the death of her son in training camp: "You must regard Marcel's passing as one of the sacrifices which the Jewish people have brought upon the altar of patriotism."[42] He counseled Jewish soldiers on their personal, military, and spiritual problems. He continually injected a Jewish content into all his actions and counsels, and for some soldiers this proved pivotal. "I want to tell you now," wrote one man stationed in France to whom Rabbi Ehrenreich had sent a prayer book, "that I was never much on religion, but I shall make it a point from now on, to read a chapter or so every night."[43] The Bernard C. Ehrenreich papers in the American Jewish Historical Society contain hundreds of letters recounting similar acts.

Michael Aaronsohn, who had interrupted his rabbinical studies to enlist in the army, recalled in his book *Broken Lights* an encounter with Rabbi Ehrenreich as "the most romantic and inspiring incident that has ever happened to me." He explained:

> It all occurred last Sunday afternoon. I was going down town and my plans were to stop at the home of Rabbi Bernard C. Ehren-

---

[38]"Report of the Jewish Welfare Board" (undated), Jewish Welfare Board File, Ehrenreich Papers.

[39]Bernard C. Ehrenreich to Verna Elsinger, 1 February 1918, World War I letters File, Ehrenreich Papers.

[40]Lillian Aldrich to Bernard C. Ehrenreich, 6 February 1918, ibid.

[41]Bernard C. Ehrenreich to J. Adelman, 5 April 1918, ibid.

[42]Bernard C. Ehrenreich to Marguerita Shokl, 28 February 1918, ibid.

[43]Sol Monsky to Bernard C. Ehrenreich, 10 February 1918, ibid.

reich for an hour or so and then to go to some dance given by a Jewish organization in this city..Upon reaching the home of the rabbi I rang the bell and someone upstairs in his flat pressed a button which opened the door. As I was walking up the stairs I heard the song "Rock of Ages". It was being sung by some folks in the home of the rabbi. I walked up the stairs happy and elated. The little daughter of the rabbi met me at the head of the stairs, greeted me very graciously. She led me into the next room and gave me a leaflet upon which the song was printed. There in the living room they were all singing—the rabbi, his wife, their son and about eight soldiers. One of these soldiers was a lieutenant, some were sergeants, and the others were privates. I immediately joined the singing. This was one of the most inspiring things I have ever witnessed. At one end of the room were the Hanukkah lights. I say to you that the real Jewish spirit was reawakened within me. I remained at the house all that evening. [44]

Aaronsohn, blinded in the Meuse-Argonne offensive, went on to become a rabbi.

Serving in organizations and attending endless meetings had not proved sufficiently rewarding to Rabbi Ehrenreich. The Camp Sheridan assignment gave him an opportunity to make a real difference in people's lives. "I spoke to our Ohio boys," wrote the mother of a deceased soldier, "and they all seem to feel that they have been forgotten by the 'folks at home' and if it would not be for Dr. Ehrenreich, Rabbi at Montgomery I do not know what would become of them. To him they look up as a father, to him they confide his [sic] troubles. When they cry, when they are homesick and all, to him they go for money and his hand is always in his pocket, never refusing one. They storm his house, nothing is refused. There is no other man like him."[45]

The intensity of the Camp Sheridan experience led Rabbi Ehrenreich to reevaluate his career. "I am really tired of the lack of re-

---

[44]Michael Aaronsohn, *Broken Lights* (Cincinnati OH, 1946) 140.

[45]Mrs. E. Shohl to editor, *The American Israelite*, February 1918. Mrs. Shohl continued: "Not Jews alone, but Gentiles wait for him to go through camp three times a day, thirty-six miles and it costs gasoline to run his car. To the sick he is always taking refreshments, it's always 'Son, what do you want?' Words cannot say what this noble man does among our Ohio boys, who have been forgotten by the three local temples, who even adopted one company."

sults that one gets in the ministry, that is the congregational ministry," he told Cyrus Adler.[46] As he mulled alternatives his mind kept returning to Camp Sheridan: "Looking after the boys of the Buckeye Division is a pleasure," he wrote. "I love them all and the response that I am receiving from them make[s] me feel that there is a vast field for work for some rabbis who are inclined to work among young men that we Jews have neglected."[47]

Beginning with Ehrenreich's experience—while still a New York University undergraduate—of helping to organize the New York City playgrounds, he developed a deepening concern for youth and for the education that would enable them to grow into responsible Jewish adults. "Education," Ehrenreich had said, "is the axis around which the earth revolves." At a time of growth in secular learning, he called for a parallel growth in Jewish learning. "We need a reawakening," he wrote. "We need a reanimation. 'The Book of Law shall not depart from out of thy mouth' must again be our motto."[48] And if education could help promote Jewish identity in general, it should more specifically help advance the Zionist cause. "We must see that we win for our holy cause, the good-will and earnest conviction of that great body of men, who, until the present, have kept distant from our faith and likewise from all that is of interest to the Jewish world." He referred to America's Jewish students: "Active and vigorous propaganda should be made to arouse in them the feeling which conditions and environments have almost deadened. From these men we should hope to gain the leaders necessary for a cause such as ours."[49] All of the causes that Ehrenreich espoused could, he believed, be best advanced by education. The restoration of interpersonal relations based on sincerity and altruism also depended upon effective education. Here again, Ehrenreich showed himself to fall in with progressive no-

---

[46]Bernard C. Ehrenreich to Adler, 3 October 1918, Cyrus Adler File, Ehrenreich Papers.

[47]Bernard C. Ehrenreich to D. Louis Grossman, 12 March 1918, World War I letters, Ehrenreich Papers.

[48]Sermon, Jewish Chautauqua, 1900, Krensky, "Gan Hadorot."

[49]"Zionism and the student," undated, ibid.

tions. As Lawrence Cremin has written, progressive education was "the educational phase of American Progressivism writ large. In effect progressive education began as Progressivism in education: a many sided effort to use the schools to improve the lives of individuals."[50] Only Ehrenreich would go farther. One could use other institutions besides schools to educate progressively.

A plan had begun to form in the Rabbi's mind before the war: why not open a summer camp dedicated to the cultivation of the mind, the body, and Jewish ideals? Encouraged by George Kohut, who had founded a similar camp, Ehrenreich diligently searched for an appropriate campsite, which he finally found in upper Wisconsin on Lake Monocqua. At first, he spent only summers at the camp, returning to his congregation in Montgomery each fall. But lengthy family separations, and the lure of Wisconsin forest land, accomplished what many congregations in other parts of the nation could not; they convinced him to leave the many friends he had made in Montgomery.[51]

At Camp Kawaga, Rabbi Ehrenreich became "Doc E." Here he felt he could fulfill his deepest wish of molding American Jewish youth. "Graduates" of Camp Kawaga included many men who went on to prominence in the Jewish community. Many echoed the sentiment of Dr. Julian Morgenstern, president of Cincinnati's Hebrew Union College, that Doc E. was an ideal man to head such a camp. "Your athletic training and outdoor interest fit you remarkably for this onerous and responsible task," he wrote. "And your strong Jewish sympathies and positive Jewish atmosphere that must pervade your camp, should make for a constructive and up-

---

[50]Lawrence Cremin, *The Transformation of the School: Progressivism in American Education, 1876-1937* (New York NY, 1961) viii.

[51]"We really have no business to be separated in this awful fashion from each other," wrote Ehrenreich. "Another year of this! Never! I could not stand it for all of Montgomery. It isn't worth it. Our future is not in what we have been, at least not in the regular congregational ministry. It is indeed high time that two people like you and I with ability and capacity and high thought begin using our God given powers for something else than we have been using them." (Ehrenreich to Irma Ehrenreich, 24 June 1919, Krensky, "Gan Hadorot," 199.) When he thrice refused a call from a major St. Louis congregation, a Montgomery newspaper commented, "He has at all times been near to his congregation and is popular with all the members and the entire citizenship of Montgomery."

building Jewish influence in the lives of all the boys who come to the camp."[52] Leon Obermayer, a Philadelphia attorney and civic leader, whom Rabbi Ehrenreich had confirmed, concurred. "As you may know, I have always thought of you as a fine man rather than a Rabbi," he wrote. "Somebody said that 'character is taught and not caught,' and with that theory in mind, I have always envied the boys in camp who came under your influence."[53]

Although Ehrenreich left Montgomery in 1921, his relationship with that city and with the state of Alabama continued. For example, after the creation of the state of Israel he served as Israeli Bond Drive chairman for Montgomery.[54] In 1971 the *Montgomery Advertiser* recalled the impressive evening service held upon the rabbi's departure fifty years before.[55] Perhaps most symbolic was the rabbi's resolve to retain his voting status as an Alabaman. "I have always regarded Alabama as my legal residence," he wrote, "and have always made that assertion and claim."[56]

Although historians note the decline of the Progressive movement after World War I, it is true that individual progressives lived on and did not give up their goals. A movement with a strong individualist orientation perhaps eventually had to disintegrate, yet it would be rash to judge the movement a failure on that account. The successful odyssey of Bernard C. Ehrenreich from an East Side child to a creative and activist student, to a cause-championing Montgomery rabbi, to a teacher and spiritual guide of young men, demonstrates the ultimate success of his form of progressivism. And his odyssey brings us as close as possible to understanding his essence.

---

[52]Julian Morgenstern to Bernard C. Ehrenreich, 3 January 1917, Camp Kawaga File, Ehrenreich Papers.

[53]Leon Obermayer to Bernard C. Ehrenreich, 23 March 1943, Leon Obermayer File, Ehrenreich Papers.

[54]*Montgomery Advertiser*, 12 November 1952.

[55]Ibid., 25 June 1971.

[56]Bernard C. Ehrenreich to Judge Leon McCord, 26 October 1936, Probate Judge, Montgomery Alabama File, Ehrenreich Papers.

5

The Sheftalls of Savannah: Colonial Leaders and Founding Fathers of Georgia Judaism

by John McKay Sheftall

A small schooner crossed the Atlantic Ocean during the stormy spring of 1733 with forty-one Jews from England on board, all hoping to gain admittance into the new British colony of Georgia. Eventually, Captain Hanson of the *William and Sarah* steered his vessel into Savannah harbor, where he and the passengers discovered a cleared bluff with a little village of wooden huts constructed by the first Georgia settlers who had arrived just five months earlier. Although the Georgia trustees in London were opposed to Jewish colonists, the Jews sought permission to settle in Savannah from James Oglethorpe, the Georgia trustee-in-residence. After an initial period of indecision, Oglethorpe granted their request.[1]

Thirty-three of the forty-one Jews on board the *William and Sarah* were of Sephardic extraction. The remaining eight—Abraham Minis and his family, Jacob Yowell, and Benjamin Sheftall and his wife Perla—were all Ashkenazic. Eight years after these Jews

---

[1]Malcolm H. Stern, "New Light on the Jewish Settlement of Savannah," *American Jewish Historical Quarterly* 52 (March 1963): 169-99; David T. Morgan, "Judaism in Eighteenth Century Georgia," *Georgia Historical Quarterly* 58 (Spring 1974): 41-54; *South Carolina Gazette* (advertisement of the *William and Sarah*) 4 August 1733.

began their struggle for economic, political, and religious survival in the wilderness of Georgia, only the Sheftalls and Minises remained in the colony. All of the others had either died or had moved elsewhere.[2]

And so it was that the middle-aged Benjamin Sheftall and his youthful wife came to establish a family in Savannah that has survived for over 250 years both in Georgia and throughout the United States. I am a member of this family. My research on Sheftall ancestry began at the age of thirteen when I knew virtually nothing of historical research or genealogy. It has actively continued. I delved into the history of the Sheftall family not only to learn about some of my more colorful ancestors, but also to explore my family's Jewish heritage. The first few generations of the Sheftalls in Savannah hold a particular fascination for me, both because of the family's uniqueness and because of its representativeness. The experiences of the immigrant, Benjamin Sheftall, were certainly original. Yet, in a sense, the accomplishments of these first two generations in Savannah are similar to experiences of other colonial Jews. Moreover, the evolution of the Sheftall family in the third and fourth generations provides insight into trends prevalent among many of America's first Jewish families.

Benjamin Sheftall was born in Frankfurt am Oder, Prussia, in 1691. Both of his sons record this fact in old family documents.[3] However, no other information about Benjamin's years in Europe was recorded. He undoubtedly left Frankfurt as a young man and traveled to London, but his motives for leaving his homeland and his time of departure remain mysteries. There is also no record of whether Benjamin made his trip alone or if others in his family came to London with him. Perhaps he lingered at some place between Prussia and England such as Amsterdam, where Jews were

---

[2]The Sheftall Diary in Keith Read Manuscript Collection, ed. by Malcolm H. Stern in "The Sheftall Diaries: Vital Records of Savannah Jewry (1733-1808)," *American Jewish Historical Quarterly* 54 (March 1965): 243-77.

[3]Mordecai Sheftall prayerbook, in the collection of Mrs. Marion Abrahams Levy, Savannah; "Levi Sheftall Autobiography," in Keith Read Manuscript Collection, ed. by Malcolm H. Stern in "Growing Up in Pioneer Savannah," *Publications of the Diaspora Research Institute* (Tel-Aviv University) Book 11, 15-22.

allowed greater freedom than in Prussia. The early vital records of
the Jewish communities in both Frankfurt am Oder and Amsterdam have disappeared as have all early records of London's Ashkenazic congregation. Despite this absence of documentation, it is
still possible to surmise that Benjamin "anglicized" his Hebrew
name after arriving in London. Apparently he assumed his father's
name "Scheftel" as a patronymic surname and further conformed
to English standards by changing the spelling of "Scheftel" to the
presently used "Sheftall."[4] He also must have met and married
Perla about 1730 or 1731.

During the winter of 1732, Benjamin and his new bride joined a
number of other London Jews who were secretly planning to sail for
the new British colony of Georgia without the consent or knowledge of the colony's trustees. Thereafter, documentation of Benjamin's life is plentiful. Records of the Georgia trustees and official
British records provide an amazingly complete story of the eventually successful Jewish settlement of Georgia. Furthermore,
shortly after the *William and Sarah* anchored at Savannah on 11 July
1733 and unloaded its contraband cargo of Jews, Benjamin began
keeping a private diary or vital record. This important manuscript
ultimately grew to contain not only a list of the Jews who traveled
to Savannah with the Sheftalls, but also births, deaths, marriages,
arrivals, and departures of the entire Savannah Jewish community
from 1733 until 1808. The original diary kept in Jeudisch-Deutsch
by Benjamin has not survived, but a full translation and continua-
tion of the document in the handwriting of his son, Levi, was preserved by the Sheftall family for many years and is now housed in
the University of Georgia Library along with many other family
papers.

Life in colonial Georgia was a struggle for any colonist. The circumstances of their arrival and colonial anti-Semitism made life
even harder for the Jews. Nevertheless, Oglethorpe did not openly

---

[4]The name "Scheftel ben Wolf" appears on a 1728 census of Jewish residents of
Frankfurt am Oder. Since "Wolf" is a substitute for the Hebrew name "Benjamin,"
it is likely that Scheftel ben Wolf was the father of Benjamin Sheftall, who would
have changed his name from "Wolf ben Scheftel" (Benjamin, the son of Scheftel)
to "Benjamin Sheftall" upon reaching England.

discriminate against the Jewish settlers. Each household head received the customary grant of fifty acres. Benjamin's land consisted of a town lot in Savannah (number four, Decker Ward), a five-acre garden lot near the town, and a forty-five-acre farm lot away from the town.[5] Benjamin and Perla built their house on the town lot, and they resided there until Perla's death in September of 1736.[6] For the next two years, Benjamin remained a widower and seems to have assumed the sole responsibility of caring for his infant son Mordecai.[7] However, just several months after the 1738 arrival of Hannah Solomons in Savannah, Benjamin married her. Hannah, a native of Amsterdam, was forty years old at the time. She made the journey to Georgia in the company of the Isaac Marks family from London.[8] Hannah's relationship to the Markses is unclear, but it is possible that a union between Benjamin and Hannah had been arranged through mutual friends or relatives before Hannah ever left Europe. After their marriage, she and Benjamin occupied his small Savannah house, and it was there that Hannah gave birth to two sons, only one of whom, Levi, survived childhood.[9]

In addition to the ownership of property, the early Savannah Jews enjoyed certain rights in Georgia that were not universally accorded to Jews. They were not inhibited by restrictions on occupation and, more important, were free to practice their religion. The Savannah Jews actually brought a Torah and circumcision box with them from London in 1733, and in July of 1735 they organized the first synagogue in the Georgia colony, K. K. Mickva Israel.[10] Worship continued in a rented structure until around 1740, when

---

[5]Charles C. Jones, Jr., *The History of Georgia* (Boston MA, 1883) 1:157-58.

[6]Sheftall Diary; *The Colonial Records of the State of Georgia,* 21:254.

[7]According to the Sheftall Diary, Mordecai Sheftall was born in Savannah on 2 December 1735. His birth followed only sixteen months after the birth of Benjamin and Perla's first child, a son, who died in infancy.

[8]Sheftall Diary.

[9]According to the Sheftall Diary, Levi Sheftall was born in Savannah on 12 December 1739. Hannah's second child, a son named Solomon, was born on 8 August 1741, and died when two years old.

[10]Sheftall Diary.

the Sephardic Jews among the group, motivated by the threat of Spanish aggression brought on by the War of Jenkins's Ear, moved away.[11] From 1741 until the late 1750s, no Jews resided in Savannah except for the Minises and Sheftalls. Despite the lack of a congregation, these two families were able to maintain their Jewish identity. Home devotions and jointly celebrated religious occasions brought the families into close contact.

The Minises and Sheftalls had more in common than friendship and an Ashkenazic heritage. Both Benjamin Sheftall and Abraham Minis began life in Savannah as farmers, but managed to establish themselves as merchants in the years that followed. Benjamin referred to himself as "storekeeper" as early as 1752.[12] Between 1755 and 1758 he expanded his business interests with numerous investments in land and goods for trade.[13] After 1760 he was consistently styled a "merchant" in every document involving him. This rather dramatic change in status reflected not only Benjamin's industry, but also the growth and development of the Georgia colony. No longer governed by trustees, but under the direct supervision of a royal governor and the London Board of Trade, Georgia was evolving rapidly into a commercial center. Benjamin merely capitalized on the abounding opportunities when he and his two sons opened their own mercantile firm to engage in trade with England and the West Indian islands.

As his economic position improved, Benjamin developed philanthropic interests. In 1750 he was one of the five founders of the St. George's (or Union) Society, an organization formed to further the education of orphan children.[14] The prestige associated with this organization was rivaled only by Solomon's Lodge, a Masonic order instituted in Georgia by James Oglethorpe. Benjamin's in-

[11]Stern, "New Light," 194-99.

[12]Colonial Conveyance Book CC-1, 57, in the collection of the Georgia Department of Archives and History, Atlanta.

[13]Various Sheftall documents recorded in Colonial Conveyance, Mortgage, Grant, Bond, and Miscellaneous Books in the collection of the Georgia Department of Archives and History, Atlanta.

[14]*Minutes of the Union Society* (Savannah, 1860) 6.

duction into Solomon's Lodge about 1758 indicates the degree to which he was accepted as a leading member of the Savannah business community. Benjamin's lambskin apron, which was worn as part of the Masonic ritual, survives as the oldest apron in the collection of Solomon's Lodge.[15]

Other than this apron, most of the personal possessions accumulated by Benjamin during his years in Savannah have not been preserved. The notable exception is a small silver salt cellar stamped with two sets of initials: those of Myer Myers, the famed colonial silversmith, and those of Benjamin and Hannah Sheftall. This heirloom (now in the collection of Mrs. Marion Abrahams Levy of Savannah) was probably purchased by the Sheftalls in the early 1760s.

Benjamin died at his home in Decker Ward on 3 October 1765.[16] He was interred about a mile from Savannah on land belonging to the Sheftall family. Six years later Hannah Sheftall was buried beside her husband.[17] Their son, Levi, erected a wall around their graves in 1773, and simultaneously established a trust for the maintenance of the plot.[18] Today the Sheftall family cemetery still exists, but vandalism and the encroachment of surrounding development have destroyed all of the eighteenth-century tombstones. A second Jewish burial ground, considerably larger than the plot enclosed by Levi, but located nearby, has fared much better. The larger cemetery was established by Benjamin's older son, Mordecai, in 1773 as a burial ground not only for his own family, but for all Savannah Jews.[19] Mordecai's cemetery, which remains visible today in the western part of Savannah, is also walled.

---

[15]*The Masonic Messenger* (May 1971) 4.

[16]Sheftall Diary.

[17]According to the Sheftall Diary, Hannah Sheftall died in Savannah on 21 February 1772.

[18]Sheftall Diary; Deed Book 200, p. 296, in the Office of the Clerk of the Superior Court, Chatham County Courthouse, Savannah.

[19]Sheftall Diary; Colonial Conveyance Book 10-2, p. 973, in the collection of the Georgia Department of Archives and History, Atlanta.

The land occupied by these cemeteries was in close proximity to the garden lot originally granted to Benjamin Sheftall by Oglethorpe. When Benjamin died, all of his property passed by will to his widow, two sons, and grandchildren. This will, which Benjamin dictated to his son, Levi, several months before his death, follows the usual eighteenth-century legal form except for the concluding remarks. After designating Hannah, Mordecai, and Levi as coexecutors of his estate, Benjamin reaffirmed his devotion to Judaism: "Resigning myself to the divine mercy of my Creator I conclude acknowledging the truth of thy Unity. Hear oh Israel that the Lord our God is one God. In thy hands I commend my Spirit. Thou hast rescued me oh Lord God of Truth."[20]

Even before Benjamin died, both of his sons had surpassed him in their accrual of wealth. Mordecai Sheftall achieved economic success as a merchant and large landowner. By the early 1760s he was actively involved in timbering, sawmilling, shipping, and retailing manufactured goods in the Broughton Street store owned by the Sheftall family.[21] Mordecai's residence was also located on Broughton Street, just a few doors from the store. It was to this home that he brought his Charleston bride, Frances Hart, in 1761.[22]

Unlike his older half-brother Mordecai, Levi Sheftall did not enter the mercantile business established by their father until the early 1760s. His first business enterprise, commenced at the age of thirteen, was dressing deerskins for a profit. This small-scale activity gradually developed into a significant tanning business. Later, as his brother's partner, Levi accumulated thousands of acres of coastal timberland and marshland, opened a sawmill, bought sev-

---

[20]Will of Benjamin Sheftall in the loose colonial records in the collection of the Georgia Department of Archives and History, Atlanta.

[21]Information concerning Mordecai Sheftall's business interests comes from Georgia Colonial Record Books in the Georgia Department of Archives and History; see also David T. Morgan, "The Sheftalls of Savannah," *American Jewish Historical Quarterly* 12 (June 1973): 348-61.

[22]According to the Sheftall Diary, Mordecai Sheftall married Frances Hart in Charleston SC on 28 October 1761. His purchase of lot seven, Heathcote Tything, Decker Ward, was recorded in Colonial Conveyance Book 10-2, 973.

eral hog farms, and invested in a cattle ranch.[23] He and Mordecai also expanded their mercantile interests by forming lucrative associations with West Indian and British firms.

Establishing and maintaining these associations occasionally necessitated personal contacts by the Sheftall brothers. Once Mordecai journeyed to London to solidify a commercial connection.[24] On another occasion, a business controversy in the West Indies resulted in Levi's decision to supervise an entire trading voyage through the Caribbean. He embarked from Savannah in 1767 on the *Two Brothers*, a thirty-ton schooner that he and Mordecai owned jointly.[25] When the twenty-eight-year-old Levi returned to Georgia a year later, he brought a fourteen-year-old bride with him. Mrs. Levi Sheftall was the former Sarah De La Motta, daughter of a Sephardic merchant on the Danish-owned island of St. Croix.[26] She and Levi immediately established their residence at the spacious two-story house he had built several years earlier on Telfair Square.[27]

In 1770 financial difficulties forced Levi to return from his mercantile activities back to the butchering and tanning business of his youth. He developed a profitable tanyard near Savannah and appears to have devoted most of his time and energy to insuring the prosperity of that enterprise.[28] Mordecai, who remained a merchant, occupied his time not only with business but also with religious and political activities. For instance, Mordecai dedicated himself to the reestablishment of the Jewish congregation in Savannah that had disbanded in his childhood. This dream became a reality in 1774 when the Sheftall and Minis families had been joined

[23]"Levi Sheftall Autobiography"; Morgan, "Sheftalls of Savannah," 348-61.

[24]*Georgia Gazette*, 24 September 1766.

[25]Ibid., 9 September 1767; Colonial Miscellaneous Bonds Book R, 266-67, in the collection of the Georgia Department of Archives and History.

[26]According to the Sheftall Diary, Levi Sheftall married Sarah De La Motta in St. Croix on 25 May 1768. Levi and his new bride returned to Savannah on 22 September 1768.

[27]"Levi Sheftall Autobiography."

[28]Ibid.

by enough Jewish families settling in Georgia to justify Mickve Israel's reformation. Because the Jews had no gathering place, Mordecai donated his own home as a place of worship, and the reorganized congregation commenced services there on 4 September 1774.[29]

Mordecai's participation in Georgia's politics began before the American Revolution and occupied an increasing amount of his time during the war itself. Unlike many more cautious merchants, Mordecai allied himself with Savannah Whigs even before independence was declared. For the next two years, he served the rebel cause in various positions of leadership. The Savannah Parochial Committee, similar to a county Committee of Safety, elected him chairman in 1775, and he held that prestigious position until 1778.[30] That same year Colonel Samuel Elbert commissioned Mordecai the Deputy Commissary General of Issues for Georgia. This appointment carried with it the rank of colonel and made Mordecai an officer on the civilian staff of the Georgia Continental Line.[31] However, furnishing Georgia's troops with supplies was a particularly difficult responsibility. Because of the shortage of public funds throughout the war, Mordecai found it necessary to purchase much of the food with his own money and extend credit to the state and federal governments. These generous loans were never fully repaid.[32]

Levi served with Mordecai on the parochial committee for several years, but the younger Sheftall seems to have viewed the clamors for independence with more skepticism than did Mordecai.[33] The first two years of the Revolution passed with little British resistance in Savannah. Georgia Whigs exercised complete control

---

[29]Ibid.

[30]*Georgia Gazette*, 16 August, 15 November 1775; "Order Book of Samuel Elbert," *Collections of the Georgia Historical Society*, 5:2:65.

[31]Papers of the Continental Congress, vol. 20, item 78, 297, in the collection of the National Archives, Washington DC.

[32]Memorial of Mordecai Sheftall to the Assembly of the State of Georgia, 12 February 1796, in the collection of the Georgia Historical Society, Savannah.

[33]*Georgia Gazette*, 15 November 1775.

over the local government, and financial leaders in the community such as the Sheftalls suffered in no dramatic way for their rebellious measures against the British government. Savannah's calm became a storm in December of 1778 when British troops launched an all-out offensive against Georgia. Most Savannah Jews, including Levi and his family, sought safety in Charleston. However, in order to carry out faithfully his job as commissary, Mordecai remained in Savannah during the ensuing siege. As a result, when the British forces captured Savannah, Mordecai and his fifteen-year-old son, Sheftall, were captured and made prisoners of war.[34]

Two years of harsh imprisonment and parole followed for the two Sheftalls. They were first housed in the Savannah guardhouse and then on board the British prison ship, *Nancy*, in the Savannah River. They were finally released on parole in the British-held town of Sunbury, Georgia. After almost a year in Sunbury, Mordecai and Sheftall escaped on a small brig with other paroled American officers only to be recaptured by a British frigate and deposited as prisoners on the British island of Antigua. Eventually the captain-general of Antigua grew lenient toward his American captives and gave them permission for a second parole. In order to comply, the Americans traveled first to New York and then to Philadelphia, where Mordecai and Sheftall were officially exchanged.[35]

During the two years of Mordecai's imprisonment, Levi supported the entire Sheftall family in Charleston. He also proved his dedication to the Whig cause on more than one occasion. The greatest test of his patriotic fervor came in the fall of 1779, when he and Philip Minis agreed to serve as guides for Count d'Estaing and the French fleet during the attempt to recapture Savannah in co-operation with American forces led by General Benjamin Lincoln.[36]

---

[34]Mordecai Sheftall's account of his capture is in the private collection of Mrs. Marion Abrahams Levy, Savannah, on microfilm at the Georgia Department of Archives and History.

[35]Affidavit of Sheftall Sheftall, 15 October 1832, in the Revolutionary Pension Papers of Sheftall Sheftall, collection of the National Archives, Washington DC.

[36]Affidavits of Philip Minis and Levi Sheftall, September 1779, published by Jacob R. Marcus, ed., in *American Jewry: Documents, Eighteenth Century* (Cincinnati OH, 1959) 266-67.

The ultimate failure of this attempt only enhanced the growing British power in Georgia. Soon even Charleston was not safe from British attack. In May 1780, while Mordecai Sheftall and his son were on their journey from Antigua to Philadelphia, the redcoats overran South Carolina's capital city.

Levi was not present when the British entered Charleston. He had left his family and fled with other male residents to Virginia. From the safety of Petersburg, he learned of the British victory. During the next few months, letters from his wife informed him of the economic hardships that his young family and his brother Mordecai's family were enduring.[37] When his wife also wrote of the death of their youngest child, Levi refused to accept his exile any longer. Not only did he feel a keen responsibility toward his family, but he probably agreed with many other Americans who thought that the British were winning the war. In August 1780, Levi took advantage of a British offer of amnesty; he returned to Charleston and swore his loyalty to the king.[38] As soon as this news reached Georgia, he was branded a Tory by former compatriots.[39]

Levi's presence in Charleston during 1780 proved fortunate not only for his own family, but also for Mordecai's wife and young children. If we are to believe tradition, it was Levi's income from a variety of business concerns that bought food and clothing for all of the Sheftalls.[40] Mordecai was also working from his Philadelphia vantage point to insure his family's safety and support. His primary goal was to enable his wife and children to join him and Sheftall in Philadelphia, and he eventually saw an opportunity to accomplish this goal. In December 1780, Congress determined to dispatch the sloop, *Carolina Packet*, to South Carolina under a flag of truce in order to take food and supplies to the destitute American

---

[37]"Levi Sheftall Autobiography"; Frances Sheftall to Mordecai Sheftall, 20 July 1780, in the private collection of Mrs. Marion Abrahams Levy, Savannah, on microfilm at the Georgia Department of Archives and History.

[38]Levi returned to Charleston prior to 10 August 1780, for on that day he transacted business with Isaac Da Costa. See the Levi Sheftall Receipt Book in the Keith Read Manuscript Collection.

[39]*Revolutionary Records of the State of Georgia* (Atlanta GA, 1908) 1:373-97.

[40]Levi Sheftall Receipt Book.

prisoners in Charleston. Through friends in Congress and at the
War Office, Mordecai secured the appointment of master of the
sloop for his son, Sheftall.[41] The mission of the *Carolina Packet*
proved successful, especially for the Sheftall family. When the
sloop returned to Philadelphia in the spring of 1781, Mrs. Frances
Sheftall and all her children were on board.[42]

The Levi Sheftall family remained in British-held Charleston
and the Mordecai Sheftall family lived in American-held Philadelphia until the end of the Revolution. However, in December 1782,
shortly after British troops withdrew from Georgia, Mordecai and
his family returned to Savannah.[43] He began immediately to re-
build his mercantile business and also started a campaign to clear
Levi of charges that he was a Tory. Mordecai, who was held in high
regard by the Savannah populace, wrote letters on Levi's behalf,[44]
efforts that did enable Levi to return with his family to Savannah
in August 1784.[45] Levi subsequently regained his Georgia citizenship and reestablished himself as a businessman. However, instead
of returning home to tanning and butchering, he concentrated his
efforts on purchasing farmland and timberland, which he developed successfully with the use of slave labor.[46]

---

[41]Richard Peters to Sheftall Sheftall, 19 December 1780, and Sheftall Sheftall to
the Georgia Delegation, 22 December 1780, in the private collection of Mrs. Marion Abrahams Levy, Savannah, on microfilm at the Georgia Department of Archives and History.

[42]Affidavit of Sheftall Sheftall, 15 October 1832, in the Revolutionary Pension
Papers of Sheftall Sheftall, collection of the National Archives, Washington DC; Papers of the Continental Congress, vol. 21, item 78, 57, in the collection of the National Archives.

[43]Sheftall Diary.

[44]Levi Sheftall to Mordecai Sheftall, 17 March 1783, in the Keith Read Manuscript Collection.

[45]*Revolutionary Records of the State of Georgia* (Atlanta GA, 1908) 3:406; Levi Sheftall Receipt Book.

[46]Information concerning Levi Sheftall's post-Revolutionary business activities
comes from deed books in the Office of the Clerk of the Superior Court, Chatham
County Courthouse, Savannah, and from papers in the Keith Read Manuscript
Collection.

Despite the charges of treason, Levi seems to have earned the trust of fellow Savannahians. In fact, prior to his death in 1809, Levi served in a number of governmental capacities: as alderman, firemaster, and United States Agent for Fortifications.[47] The latter position was one of great responsibility, for Levi was personally in charge of the construction and maintenance of all federal fortifications within Georgia.[48] Mordecai also held civic positions in the years between the Revolution and his death in 1797. At various times he served as city magistrate, warden, inspector, and state legislator.[49] Both Sheftall brothers were also instrumental in the post-Revolutionary reorganization of Mickve Israel in 1786.[50] Levi served as a trustee for the congregation for a number of years, and he was president when the congregation received its charter from the Georgia governor in 1790.[51]

There is no doubt that Mordecai and Levi were recognized as community leaders in their latter years. At their deaths, each left behind small financial empires and legacies of their philanthropy. There were also sons and daughters to inherit the family wealth and enjoy the social position that the first two generations of Sheftalls had obtained. Despite a few minor squabbles, Mordecai and Levi's offspring (the third generation of Sheftalls in Savannah) remained a closely knit family. With their spouses and children, they constituted a majority of the Mickve Israel congregation. They also dominated the medical and legal professions in Savannah. Mor-

---

[47]*Georgia Gazette*, 4 July 1799, 20 August 1801; Levi Sheftall letters and other documents in the Secretary of War Papers, National Archives, Washington DC.

[48]Among other projects, Levi oversaw the construction of Fort Jackson in Savannah and Fort Hawkins on the Ocmulgee River near the future site of Macon GA.

[49]*Georgia Gazette*, 19 March 1789, 4 March 1790; Sheftall Diary; Mordecai Sheftall letters and other documents in the Mordecai Sheftall Family Papers, American Jewish Historical Society Library, Waltham MA, and in the private collection of Mrs. Marion Abrahams Levy, Savannah, on microfilm at the Georgia Department of Archives and History.

[50]Records of Congregation Mickve Israel in the collection of the congregation, Savannah.

[51]Sheftall Diary; Minute Book of Congregation Mickve Israel, 1790-1851, in the collection of the congregation, Savannah.

decai's son, Sheftall, and Levi's sons, Benjamin, Mordecai, and Emanuel, became lawyers, while Mordecai's son, Moses, and Levi's sons, Abraham and Solomon, studied medicine and established lucrative practices in Savannah.[52]

The first three generations of Savannah Sheftalls were united by their dedication to Judaism and their physical proximity. However, in the fourth and fifth generations this important unity began to crumble. Some of Levi's grandchildren married outside the Jewish faith, and other family members left Savannah for New York, Philadelphia, California, and Texas. As assimilation into the Christian community continued in the mid and late nineteenth century, various branches of the family were ostracized and legal conflicts erupted. Family letters, legal documents, and oral tradition chronicle the unhappy results of this interfamilial conflict.

This slow splintering of unity within the Sheftall family was not atypical of what many early American Jewish families experienced to some degree. Initial struggles for economic and religious survival encouraged cohesion, but after the efforts of the first several generations brought financial security and sometimes even political recognition, cultural and religious assimilation often followed. As the younger family members identified with the Christian community through marriage or other social ties, older family members usually reacted by severing all contact. Offspring from these mixed unions typically had little association with their Jewish relatives. My own branch of the Sheftall family, although not practicing the Jewish religion for more than 150 years, was unusual in that it preserved knowledge of its Jewish heritage.

Today Benjamin Sheftall's family numbers about one thousand and covers the United States. Only a few family members are practicing Jews. Moreover, many Sheftall descendants—some even living in Savannah—have little knowledge that their ancestors were among Georgia's first Jewish settlers. This lack of knowledge is to me unfortunate. All of us—and the descendants of every other early American Jewish family—share a common heritage of which we should be aware and in which we should take great pride.

---

[52]Sheftall Papers in the Keith Read Manuscript Collection.

6

Reminiscences of Joseph Joel in Europe and America

by Myron Berman

This memoir is a portion of the autobiographical manuscripts written by Joseph Joel (1882-1960) of Richmond, Virginia. Mr. Joel's father, Salomon Czaczkes (Joel) immigrated from Galicia in the Austro-Hungarian Empire to the United States. Unlike the vast majority of east European immigrants, Salomon Joel and his family eventually returned to Europe, their passage back home being paid by their European relatives. Joseph Joel was an infant when he arrived in the United States, and what he knew of his background was a result of oral tradition.

Although his father had been a grain merchant in Europe, Salomon Joel operated a jewelry store in Richmond. He was not successful, and after moving several times within Richmond, he finally settled in Chicago in 1893. When economic conditions in the United States worsened shortly afterwards, Salomon Joel returned to Europe. He died there, and many members of his family were later massacred by the Nazis.

Joseph Joel returned to the United States in 1914 and, after a brief sojourn in New Mexico, he became a jewelry merchant in Richmond. He achieved greater success than his father. He married Minnie A. Weinstein. Their only son, Captain Milton Joel, was killed during World War II. When Joseph Joel settled in Richmond, there were approximately 1,000 Jews living there and worshiping at the three synagogues. Beth Shalome, the oldest, had roots in the eighteenth century and was known as the Portuguese Synagogue. It eventually merged with Beth Ahabah, the largest congregation, whose German constituency was composed mainly of immigrants and first-generation Americans. Kenesseth Israel, the Polish Synagogue that

had been founded in the 1850s, completed the trio. Joel also describes the organi-
zation of a fourth house of worship for immigrants, the Sir Moses Montefiore, or
the Russian Synagogue.

The Joseph Joel manuscripts are owned by Mrs. Julian Jacobs of Richmond, Jo-
seph's niece. This selection from the larger body of manuscripts appears in Mr.
Joel's choice of words and grammatical usage.

Although my only child is no more among the living, I write the
memoirs of my life to him. I have to do so, for if I don't write them
to him, they will not be written. If I want to write them, I have to
write them to someone, and he alone, though dead, is the one I can
write to. His body may be dead, but he is not dead to me. I think
often of him. I think of him frequently and whenever I do I don't
feel as if he is dead but very much alive. I cannot, for some reason,
believe him to be dead.

This urge to write, to talk to him, is a need to do something. It's
a consolation by reminding myself of the past. It's a pleasure. I
often treat myself to this kind of a treat when I sit down in my arm-
chair in my den and when I get in bed nights. Bringing forth scenes
of the past is deep pleasure. Why, what foolish things and happen-
ings and scenes come to life. Beautiful ones, foolish ones, com-
mendable ones, and ones I can be ashamed to tell. It's nice, try it.
Recall the past of childhood, teen age, later ones, and so on even of
but recently. The foolish things that gave pleasure. The ones I worried foolishly over.

What destiny these memoirs will have I can't foretell but I feel
they will be burnt up or go in the trash can with all the other collected manuscripts, papers, books I have. I don't know of a single
relative of mine, I mean of both sides of the family, my nephews
and nieces, that have my taste of culture. They like boogy-woogy—
that new type of *tanzen* and *gringen*. They sit glued to a television
for hours, watching some no count jumping around. What they
read is magazines, never a classical book. They are well versed
what actress is changing her husband and such stuff. Yes, this will
not be of value to them but I am deriving pleasure talking to my boy.
Should I retain my senses before I pass on, I will give them to Ellen
(Elaine), my daughter-in-law. She, I feel, will appreciate it. She
knows me beyond my looks. She followed my thinking way. Or I

will destroy them and my other collections, myself, as well as all the letters from my father and my son and my friends. I am the third child. My father's name was Sheloime or Salamon Czaczkes. He was the oldest of eight children. He was born, either by Tarnopol or Podwoloczyska, which belonged to Austria then. That section was known as Galicia, formerly belonging to Poland. My grandfather, my father's father, I think was named David. David, I used to hear that he resided in Tarnopol and used to travel with merchandise to the large European markets like Leipzig, etc., in Germany and Yarmalinetz-Berditschef in Russia. My father, too, used to go to these markets but not with merchandise. My grandfather went there with his goods to sell like a caravan, instead of camelpacks, they used peasant horse-drawn wagons. There weren't trains in those days.

Of my grandmother (father's mother) I don't know a thing. I don't know of her people. Where she came from, where she is buried, or even her name. She must have died young for my father was an orphan in his teenage. It's a shame that I didn't have sense to want to know more of my people. You see they brought me to the U.S. when a child of two. I was torn away from them and grew up unattached to them. All I know of my grandmother of my father's side is that she died in her early life and nothing more. Not her name—nor when she died, how she died, where she is buried and not even her maiden name. My father, I know, was one of eight children which names I will list separately and their children and all about them as much as I know. The eighth child was from the second wife.

The eight names and in rotation, as far as I know, are:

Chana Pessie married Peisse Leibeles
Gitze, Minnie's grandmother
Shloime—my father
Rive—the Turkels are from her branch
Chaie—the Zimring's grandmother
Hersch—the famous Herman Joel
Moische—who died
Yosche—Uncle Joe the banker, who was but a half brother

I remember hearing that when the railroad was opened, my grandfather settled in Podwoloczyska, a Russian-Austrian frontier city. He lived somewhere here near the river and the bridge. There was the city—but only a few houses. As a child, I wasn't interested to know where it was. I don't know which of the children were born there. Of those days, I know but two things. One is that when my Aunt Gitzie Rashbaum—She married a Rashbaum, who he was—where he came from I don't know. I do know this—that he was a learned man and a maskil, i.e., a person who joined the enlightened movement, who wanted to know secular knowledge. He was off and on in the world. He played the stockmarket which was something for those days and that he was often off his horse and my father had to put him back on his feet. They lived high. Well the main thing is that when his Gitze got married, the wedding was in the tavern. I recollect the tavern. They had to have it there for the rooms of the homes those days were small and everybody in town, Jew-friend-Christians and family and friends out of town had to be invited and they came.

It wasn't like now. One sends a gift and doesn't give a damn. We haven't now the family feelings—the closeness—the warmness is lost. Those days, if there was a Simchele like a Brith-Bar mitzvah, tenaim, i.e., engagement and weddings, even a funeral, it was something. It was everybody's. So they had to have a spacey place, like now, they have affairs here at hotels in NY in special halls. Well, they had it in the tavern and in the middle of the merry-making they learned that the Hulans are coming to see the wedding, so my grandfather dispatched the bride through a secret hole of the big fireplace through a secret passage which led to a nearby village for safety and the other women ran home.

You see Podwoloczyska was the Austrian frontier city. Wolocyzska, the Russian side. The Hulans were cavalry stationed to guard on one side, i.e., the Austrian. (There are several hills and I knew and saw one of these formerly secret entrances to the hills, which led, I don't know where to.)

Some friendly peasant brought the news to my people that the soldiers are coming to watch the wedding. We Jews knew the goim. They had to be treated to drinks and eats which we Jews never mind. But we also know that a goy these days wasn't civilized. He had to get drunk and when drunk, he will want to dance with the bride and the other women and lose control of himself, start fighting and raping. So they dispatched the women to safety and with bribes to some higher officer, the soldiery were called back to the barracks and everything went on peacefully.

The second thing I know is that my father was for his age, enlightened. It was then a general movement—maskilim were everywhere except the Chassidim. These were three types of people—Chassidim, Maskilim and Zionists. The first aliyas started then. Russia was treating Jews badly and as there was a Russian national liberal movement which they called nihilist, the enlightenment brought self-respect to the Maskilim, the younger Jews who began to leave Russia. Most of them went to the U.S. but some went to Palestine and these we call the first Aliyah.

My father was young then—he was a Bocher, i.e., a young man who studies. Where he studied, where he stayed, I don't know, but I do know that my grandfather remarried a woman who we called Bube Raize and she was so darn mean to him that he [i.e., my father] just couldn't stand her any more and he picked himself up and walked to Stanislow, which is a good size city in the Bukovina and which had a famous Yeshiva. A Yeshiva is a place where Torah in advanced stage is taught. If a Yeshiva is famous it doesn't mean that it had to be a large school like Harvard. No, in such cases it means that an exceptional learned teacher is there, who can expound passages better than others, so the place is famous and scholars flock there to sit at his feet and hear him. His midrashim, his interpretations, are treasured. Notes were made and kept but most of these notes, I am sorry to say, were lost. We Jews were always chased around; who had a mind to drag with him in his wanderings such notes. To save their lives was of more interest.

Well this Bube Raize, who was my grandfather's second wife and my Uncle Joe's mother. Where he picked her up I don't know. She was Russian, was at heart a very pious and a very charitable soul, but a mean stepmother. One of the kind that is always at you so [my father] he picked himself up and became a real Yeshiva Bocher. Ate every day at someone's table, every day it was at a different one, slept on a hard bench in schul or on somebody's chairs. Yes, that is the way they lived, that was the mitzvah people had though they were poor themselves, to help the boys to sustain themselves and to study Torah.

When my father I think was sixteen, yes sixteen years old, she (my father's stepmother) made a schidach, i.e., a match with a niece of hers, a brother's child in Proskurov, Russia. The old lady did not mean the Hagadah, as she meant the knedlach. She helped her poor brother who had a house full of daughters and only one son to get rid of one of his girls without a dowry. So they made this match, sight unseen, and my father used to tell me, when I was old enough to understand him, that my mother was but eleven years old and when he came to the Tenoim, i.e. engagement, they had to drag her forth from behind the stove—Dutch type of a heating oven made out of mud and flint rocks, reaching almost to the ceiling and she hid herself for bashfulness behind this oven. My father showed off his learning of Torah and of Datchkeit which means secular knowledge, as he spoke and read German and Polish. How well, I can't say. I don't think he knew it good but better than the guests, the judges. He went back to the Yeshiva and came back and married. He was at the prescribed and recommended age of eighteen. She fourteen.

My father was like I was. He used to like to talk to me about his past and present troubles and I used to do the same with my son, that is why I know of his life. Why I don't know more of his father and nothing of his mother, I can't explain. She must have passed on while he was young.

My grandfather lived in Podwoloczyska. Dealt in grain but was buried in Tarnopol, his former home. His second wife lived on in Podwoloczyska. I remember her well, and as I said, the Bube Raize, she was a very good woman. She buried the poor—saw that the orphans are cared for—married off all the poor maids, young and old—saw the poor, had everything for Pesach. She wasn't ashamed and even went to the common house to schnor a nice nedove [i.e. donation] from the manager, or proprietor and the girls and often to help console some newcomer. Some Jewish girl who got in trouble and knew no other way to hide her shame than to go to the nearest whorehouse, who saw to it that she is transferred to some other common place far from her hometown. Those poor girls are the most unfortunate ones and deserve our pity instead of our resentment, for they weren't modern like the present time girls and they did not know how to protect themselves and this Bube Rezy did for them what she could, which at best was but a consoling word. She couldn't take her out and marry her off as kacher as a virgin. So the poor thing remained a pleasure giving thing for the schone Yidden, who wanted a change from his Metziah that he got in his marriage deal.

My father's Ketubah, i.e., marriage contract, I haven't. This, too, got lost in wandering—coming to America—returning to Europe-Russia, when he entered Galicia in World War I, rounded up all Jews, packed the old and sick on springless peasant carts and made the young and healthy ones march on foot to Siberia. I have this letter of this wandering. Later on he moved to Vienna, then to Lemberg. So this is how family papers—rare books and other treasured mementoes—got lost and this is how our Jewish treasures got lost and so lost in our wandering. Just imagine what treasure of Jewish interest got lost in our days, in Hitler's time in Russia, Poland, Germany, etc. Who cared to save them? The old ones who had them and knew of these mementoes, these manuscripts, these rare books, died or were exterminated and all these treasures of knowledge got lost. Many an unpublished commentary got lost, and they were, perhaps, exceptional good ones. Many a young person did not know that his father possessed rare mementoes or books; for the younger generation was only interested in modern literature, so things were left behind and destroyed by the Germans or Poles who occupied the Jewish homes.

When my father married, as I said, he was young, only eighteen. My mother, I think fourteen. As customary, he ate kesst, i.e., a custom that time. The young folks were given time and opportunity to ripen. The daughter was shown and taught wifely duties—to take care of the house, cook, mend and to observe kashrus which means to run a home in a Jewish way. The son-in-law, in this case, my father, was given the opportunity, too, but as he was an Austrian and a young man who was in various cities, so called modern ones, where they had wooden floors, where they spoke German, and as he was the son of an international trader not an innkeeper (my mother's father had a little inn and they lived in the back of it). The floors were of hard clay. They cooked in the front of the baking oven on a tripod which caused the food to smell and taste of smoke (while in my father's environment, they cooked on a regular stove). So he was looked up to, instead of as a younger who has to be shown and he did show them. It didn't take him long. He found himself likeable, enlightened friends, businessmen and he became a businessman. I don't know the year he married but I do know he came to the U.S. in 1884. He had to leave Russia. Russia was persecuting her Jews and refused to extend permission for my father as an Austrian, to reside in Proskurov. So he emigrated to the U.S. and if I don't forget, I'll tell you an interesting thing which caused him to go to the U.S. and you will, if not already, begin to believe in fate. He was also thinking of going to Palestine.

I know this, we were three children when we came to the States. My sister, Fanny, who was the oldest one and who died of consumption at the age of nineteen. She died on the second day of Chalomoed [the week of] Pesach. She is buried in Sir Moses Montefiore Cemetery, Sec. M I on April the 26th 1891, born 1873.

My brother Moses, I had two brothers by the name Moses. My half brother was named after my older brother. They are both dead. Well, this older brother was born, as my sister, in Proskurov, Russia. He was born in 1877, went to school in Richmond, worked at various things while we lived in Chicago during the World's Fair and when we returned in 1894 to Podwoloczyska, he was employed as an English correspondent for various egg exporters. Then he traveled to Germany, England, Scotland and other places as a salesman for Meier Ehrlich Exporter. My brother was tubercular. Those days many people were afflicted with this disease, especially abroad. He died while visiting home in 1904. He, as my mother, are buried in Podwoloczyska. His real name was Moses Leib Czaczkes.

I was the third child. I was born on the 31st of December, 1881, old style as I too, was born in Proskurov, Russia as an Austrian. I have the birth certificate which makes it, January 12, 1882. I somehow got mixed up figuring out the old calendar to the new one and celebrate my birthdays on the 13th of January n. style.

After me, came my brother, Israel. Then my sister, Esther, then my brothers, Herman, Ephraim, then Robert, then two small girls who died in their infancy. Then my half brother Moses and our half sister, Clara. About myself and brothers and sisters I'll tell you later, but now, I want to tell you about my mother which isn't much.

Her name was Ite or Yetta, born in Proskurov, Russia, about 1854 or 1855. I don't think these dates are correct. I don't think she was twenty-seven years old when I was born, the third child. She died and was buried in Podwoloczyska, Austria. (One was born before Robert and one before Mushke from the second wife) the second day Rosh Hashanah, 1900. She was a good mother, never fussed. She was always ailing. Some stomach trouble and those days, they didn't know about dieting. The poor woman was either cooking or mending or darning stockings and socks. Of her father, I told you. He and her mother were plain old-type Russian Jews. He went to schul twice a day and between times, he either ate, slept or waited on some peasant with a drink of Vodka or a glass of chi which is tea. My grandmother did the same. She either cooked, darned, mended, read in her Veiberischen Teitsch, which means her woman's prayer book or also waited on some muzik, i.e., Russian peasant. They had six daughters and one son—a good crop. All lived. I knew them. I'll try to write about them later.

My mother was the oldest. I remember sitting as a child in her lap when she was in the rocking chair and she told me stories. One I recalled clearly. About her coming over in a sailboat and that an octopus wrapped his tenticles around the sails ready to turn the boat over and to feed on the passengers. I don't remember how they were saved. Yes, it's very little of her life I can tell. It was the same drudgery, day in and day out. She went nowhere except Rosh Hashana, Yom Kippur to schul. The poor woman walked from 1st Street, West Broad to Eleventh Street Schul or Mayo Street. It was Sir Moses Montefiore Schul. Well let me tell you about my father and from his life, much will be known of the others. I told you about my father's youth. About his marriage. Now I will begin of his life as a married man.

By being himself a well-versed man in Torah and Hebrew, he read much of then just appearing Hebrew literature in newspaper and magazine form. As is said at that time, the Maskilim appeared in Russia and in Germany. It was the time of the Jewish Renaissance. The time when all these Jewish writers appeared. The time when modern Zionism sprouted. This brought him into a circle. Though himself a young man, yet of older people, learned and wise, cultured and religious. He moved about in all circles. He

could sit in schul evenings and argue about someone's interpretation of a passage in the Torah as he could sit in his home or at some
friends' [house] arguing about politics, Zionism or some other Jewish question or philosophy. He nor his friends were scholars but
they knew plenty of rubbing shoulders and talking about things
and worthwhile subjects. In those days, you were either one of
three types of a Jew. The Klause man (hassid), who did not want to
know anything but Torah and who did not accept any liberal-
minded or modern interpretation. Then there was the plain gruber
jung, i.e., the ignorant. The poor boy who had to go to work and
had no time to spare for study, and the Maskilim, the enlightened
one who read everything, who wanted to know about everything
and who feared not to trim his beard, to smoke a cigarette on Sab-
bath or to drink tea of the Samovar that the Schikse has just made.
They did these things not publicly, but in their homes, for they were
sensible people. They did not want to show off their modernism. In
this way, he made a lot of friends, and I think through these associations, he became a businessman. I know he had a distillery and
from its by-product, a yeast plant, and as he had to buy grain for
his own need, he dealt in grain too.

My father wasn't a rich man but nobody was in that little town.
He was as well off as any of the other citizens, i.e., he had a nice
home. There were always people of all walks of life going in and
out. Business transactions were made there and matters of all kinds
were discussed. All I know of those days is of hearing, talking of
his past. My mother never kept up to him. She was like all women
those days. The average ones, ignorant. He didn't expect of her
anything else but to have children, run the house.

In the Eighties [1880s] Russia started to persecute the Jews. She
tried to get rid of them, and as my father was a foreigner, he had to
get out. As long as bribery was taken he stayed, but the time came
where it was so bad that the Jews who could get out didn't care to
remain in Russia. Many went to the U.S., some to Palestine, South
America. My father went to the U.S. and to Richmond, Virginia,
because he had here a sister, Gitze Rashbaum, and his single
brother, Hersch or Herman.

Before I continue about his life in the U.S., I want to tell you
about them. My aunt Gitze Rashbaum lost her husband. She was

left a widow with four daughters, two sons. She lived in Tarnopol, Galicia. As long as her husband was alive, they lived very nicely, but when he passed on, they were left very poor and nothing in Tarnopol for them to do but to sit around and be supported by the family; and it was my father who did it as he was the only one who could do a little for them. So my Aunt went to Vienna hoping that there the children could find employment. Why they didn't stay in Vienna as thousands of other Jews did, I don't know. I know they went from Vienna to Belgium and from there to the U.S. I think as immigrants supported by the Jewish Welfare Association that was then functioning, helping the wave of emigrations.

In those days, the immigrants were handled worse than cattle. They were not transported by the fastest and directest route, but by the worst. I know what I am talking. The welfare agents, those Yidlach were on the jobs to make a living—not to be helpful to the travelers. Yes, the association was but not the machers, the workers. They forwarded the people by the most cheapest way and this way by the slowest and indirect. They were laid over awaiting groups for days at some place. They were sent in freight ships which made stops at several ports. The Versorgers did this, because they got a kickback from the cheap ship companies. Well, my aunt Rashbaum was in one of them with the pecklach and her asset, the children. Those days, children that were of age to go to work were an asset. Those days, whatever every child earned was the mother's in this case. The children those days didn't know of pocketmoney or its theirs. Well, the agency sent them to Virginia and Richmond, for in those days, America advertised for immigrants. Virginia did too, so they went to Richmond.

From Belgium, they went to England, London, and in London, Uncle Herman on their station was one of the London Versorgers, and in checking the names of the various passengers, he came upon hers—Rashbaum—which he knew was also his sister's name whom he hadn't seen for many, many years; and after looking into this case, they discovered that they were the lost forgotten brothers and sisters. So he, too, decided to go along to the U.S., Richmond and they travelled from hereon, i.e., London together. That Uncle Herman was the youngest child of the first set of children, and as an orphan, he learned to be a watchmaker, roamed around the world of whom I'll tell you more later.

I don't know anything of their trip and their getting settled in Richmond. I'll have to skip all this, but I will tell you what I know of them as a child later.

I remember her having a store in 17th Street East where she sold to coloured and farmers as it was the old market section—old suits and other things by the line. That time readymade dresses were unknown. Some of the children worked. They made a living. Suddenly they moved to Baltimore, no doubt, the place looked to them as a better opportunity for the children. They were all grown up. In fact, the oldest one, Rosa, was already married. She came here with her husband. Their name was Parriles (Paril). My aunt had six children: four girls, two boys: Rosa, Sarah, Josephine, Clara, Henry, Leopold. Of these, there still is the one alive, Sarah Sneidman, residing in Hartford, Conn.

When my father came to Richmond, he came here reluctantly, disheartened, without money, without a trade, no shopkeeping experience. He just didn't know what to do. His brother and sister weren't rich. Help from strangers he didn't want to accept so you can understand how downhearted he felt. Anyhow, they, I think it was his brother, Herman, rented him a small store on the corner of 8th & Broad (south east corner) right next to the Old Murphy Hotel. That time both places were a frame two-story building with small window panes. They hired then a Jewish boy, a son of old man Harris or Harrison, and my father opened shop. He lived in the back part of the store and slept upstairs. I think that jewelry store or rather watch repair shop barely brought in a living, for my father kept on moving about from section to section, blaming the locality, not himself. He was to blame for he did not try to learn a trade and at least try to earn what it cost him to hire a repair man.

We lived for a few years here, then we moved to 1503 East Main—then West Broad near Brook Avenue where I started school, Lea Street. Then we moved to South Richmond which was then Manchester somewhere on the west side of the thirteenth hundred block Hull Street. Then to the 1800 block East Main and then to Chicago in 1902. At 1503 East Main, my brother Israel and my sister Esther were born; in Manchester, my brother Herman, and in Chicago, my brother Ephraim.

It was during the World's Fair that my father thought there in Chicago, his Mazel will become active. Why I don't know. He didn't know a trade. He had no money. He didn't want to be a shamos or Hebrew teacher like many other unfortunate middle age people fell back on. Why he went to Chicago, I don't know. He wasn't a venturesome man who liked to rove and always do something else. In fact, he liked to do nothing but read or go around with some schaliach to collect for some cause. This is why he didn't make a living in Richmond. For he was always giving his time to Jewish civic matters—like organizing the Sir Moses Montefiore Schul. First it was but a minyon over a flat on East Main St.—getting the people to attend, so that there will be a minyan to pray. To bother with bringing down a Schohet who was Mr. Gerson. His children still reside in Richmond. He is the one who organized the Sir Moses Montefiore cemetery and who buried the dead. Yes, he gave his time to such things instead of trying to stay at the store and to repair a watch.

When my father arrived in Chicago, I remember it was on a Friday evening. It wasn't Schabbath but almost. No one met us. You see, Uncle Herman was there. He, too, went to Chicago from Europe. Whether my father wanted to save the streetcar fare or not, I don't know. All I remember, we children, five of us and my father and poor Mother walked, shlepping our pecklech to the boarding house where my Uncle boarded. It was a Jewish place with many boarders. The boarders didn't have a room for themselves. Many of them slept in one room. It was Friday evening—I cannot recollect where we slept, where we ate. I only remember living on the second floor of a brick house on Banker Street where my brother Ephraim was born and I became Bar Mitzvah.

I remember that my father started to peddle jewelry from house to house and didn't like it and couldn't make a go at it. He opened a store which was half jewelry and half grocery. How he did it or who helped him to it, I don't know, undoubtedly Uncle Herman. His brother must have spent his savings. My brother, Moses, started working first in some sweatshop making cigars, and I think there it was that he got consumption. Later he worked with Uncle

Herman who was a watchmaker in a jewelry store in the Italian section. Went to school, to cheder and as I said, I was Bar Mitzvah. There was no affair.

My father, I want to tell you when he arrived in the U.S., became a pious Sabbath-observing Jew. We drank stale tea—ate rewarmed or cold dishes. He didn't permit us children to use soap on Shabbath so our hands and necks weren't too clean looking. Yes, as he was non-observant in Russia, he made up in America, we children carried [not] even a handkerchief in our pocket. We had it wrapped around our wrist or tucked into our pants around the waist. He became here meshuga from this keeping close the Shabbath. Running around all day attending to Yiddische things, I think was the why he did not make a living and even during the Chicago fair. After the closing of the fair, we returned to Galicia. My Uncle Joe, my father's brother, sent us the fare. I think my mother's parents helped him with a little. Yes, everybody from the states used to and still do send ticket or passage money for folks to come here, but in my father's case, that poor man was so mazeldik for him, things were reverse, him they sent passage money from Europe. I can take a bet if it would be done, to check it, that in the history of emigration, this case is the only one whom they sent money. However, this calls for a separate section. I have to tell you how we knocked about in Chicago before leaving. In Brooklyn, before taking ship-experience on board-London, Hamburg, Europe, and our arrival at Podwoloczyska, passing Tarnopol.

I told you that my father was no businessman. Even in those days, where opportunities were plenty, he just couldn't see them and had to go back to Europe, i.e., Austria, a poor man with six children. He went to Podwoloczyska because there his rich brother Joseph lived and because Podwoloczyska was the Austrian frontier city where he thought he will be able, with financial help of his brother, to go back in the grain etc. business, which he did. Somehow my poor father was a schlemiel despite the fact he was a well-read man in secular matters. He had a searching and analytic mind. He always read newspapers to be posted of current events, but also research literature, mostly, of course, relating to Jewish matters. For in his days, the Jews just began to write about Reformism. I don't mean that stuff whether we should or not wear a Talis or omit a certain prayer. I mean social—also about Zionism. That social question was a hot topic because Jews native of the U.S. of America did not enjoy it. He would have made a good teacher. He just wasn't a business man.

When he received the passage fare, the first thing I remember he moved himself, with his brood, over to some landsman, a Mr. Gelbert, an egg dealer in Chicago. Here we lived a few weeks. Why, I don't know. He could have gone on to Europe. Then we went to Brooklyn and here, too, we squatted with some landsman who had a piece of a cork factory, i.e., he would buy up all discarded corks. Those days all drinks came corked, trim off the outside and resell them. He lived in a long, deep store in Brooklyn. In the front were a couple of machines which peeled off the outsides of the corks and in the rear, the manufacturer lived and here, my father piled himself in. My deceased brother and I who were the older boys went to sleep every night with some young man who had a room. Whether or not we slept in beds, I don't know, likely not.

Here we stayed a few days then we took ship. Of course, we went steerage, and steerage those days, sixty years ago, was steerage. All we ate because we lived kosher, was herring and potatoes cooked in the shell. Wurst, that we brought along, tea and black bread. Even in the arranging of this passage, my father showed his business abilities like hanging around with his landsleute and not taking a direct-going boat. That freighter went to England. We and our pecklech were removed from the large boat to rowboat, taken to London. There we hung around a day, I think at the railroad station. Then we went by a freighter to Hamburg. That little freighter was a hell hole. We slept in it only—couldn't stay inside—and the rough sailors moved among us called us anti-Jewish names and such. I don't know how long this trip lasted. We lived on cheese that my father bought in London—wurst and tea. From Hamburg to Podwoloczyska. The trip was good. It was springtime. We enjoyed travelling through, we went 1st class. Germany, in Austria at Tarnopol, Uncle Herman met us at the station. He was back too, already. No one else, though, we had plenty close relatives. I think it was due because the poor Amerikaner, not a regular one came back.

We arrived in Podwoloczyska early morning and only Moische Leib, my Uncle Joe's son, awaited us. We were led down to Uncle Joe's place, who himself lived in but two rooms and a kitchen. His family consisted of four children; his wife and an old mother and in this crowd, we were piled in. I don't know where we slept. It wasn't long we moved into a newly furnished adobe-type house of also two rooms and kitchen. Uncle Joe supported us—got my father a partner and my father became a grain dealer which included everything in this line, wheat, rye, all kinds of peas, beans, all seeds, etc. He somehow managed to make a meager living. Several times he went broke, and Uncle Joe found him a new partner and he gave him money to operate until we, the children, got older and helped him along. I resided in Breslau, Germany, Israel-Danzig. We sold direct or Herman travelled in Russia buying direct. Father at this stage, was going satisfactory. Had his own home, lived nicely, etc.

Then World War I broke out, where he and all the others couldn't do business any more. Jews were moved to Russia by foot to the interior, supposedly to Russia, excusing this act because the Jews were pro-German. When they were liberated, due to world intervention, the family went to Vienna and when the war ended, they went back to Lemberg where he passed away in 1935. All during the war, he couldn't do any business so the children had to support him, which wasn't pleasant. After his death, his second wife, and my sister, Clara, came to Richmond.

7

Eugenia Levy Phillips:
The Civil War Experiences
of a Southern Jewish Woman

by David T. Morgan

War causes dislocation and misery in unpredictable ways—
oftentimes to the unsuspecting civilian as well as to the soldier in
the front lines. Women, far from the fields of battle, have been
known to become involved indirectly and to suffer because of their
involvement. And so it was during the Civil War with Eugenia Levy
Phillips who, probably more than any other Southern woman of
prominent political connections and high social standing, paid a
heavy price in humiliation and suffering for her abiding loyalty to
the Confederacy. Here is a bizarre story, the story of a woman who
seems to have courted trouble by refusing, in the words of her husband, to be discreet in expressing her convictions.

Eugenia Levy Phillips was the daughter of Jacob C. Levy and
Fanny Yates Levy. She was born in Charleston, South Carolina, in
1820. Her father, also a native of Charleston, was a well-educated
man and a successful merchant. He was director of the Union In-
surance Company from 1830 to 1840, a delegate to the Knoxville
Railroad Convention in 1836, and a member of the Charleston
Chamber of Commerce from 1841 to 1847. Although a thorough-
going Southerner, he was a Union Democrat who opposed nullifi-

cation and secession. In 1848 he moved to Savannah, Georgia, where he lived until his death. Eugenia's mother was from Liverpool, England.[1]

On 7 September 1836, at age sixteen, Eugenia was married in Charleston to Philip Phillips, a lawyer who had served in the South Carolina legislature and had stood forthrightly and firmly against the doctrine and ordinance of nullification in 1833. Following his term in the legislature, he had moved in 1835 to Mobile, Alabama, where he established a thriving legal practice. Not long after the wedding in 1836, Eugenia and her new husband left Charleston, heading for Mobile by railway, stagecoach, and riverboat.[2]

For nearly eighteen years Philip and Eugenia Phillips lived in Mobile. Their first house was in the western suburbs; their second was on the bay. Fire destroyed the house on the bay, along with nearly all the family's possessions. By this time Phillips, as attorney for the Bank of Mobile and an established lawyer handling 150 to 200 cases a year, enjoyed a handsome annual income of $8,000, and so the family recovered quickly from the disaster and continued to do well. In 1853, when Eugenia and Philip left Mobile, they had seven children and one on the way. Clavius, Fanny, Caroline (called Lina), Salvadora, Eugene, John Walker, and John Randolph were all born in Mobile between 1838 and 1850. William Hallett and Philip were born in Washington in 1853 and 1855 respectively.[3]

Philip Phillips had been a political activist in South Carolina, and so he was in Alabama. His involvement in politics led him to the chairmanship of the Alabama Democratic party, two terms in the state legislature in 1844 and 1851, and finally to a term in the United States House of Representatives in 1853. One term in Congress at an annual salary of less than one-third of what he was accustomed to making as a lawyer prompted him to refuse to stand

---

[1]Barnett Abraham Elzas, *The Jews of South Carolina* (Philadelphia PA, 1905) 194; Elizabeth H. Jervey, "Marriage and Death Notices from the *City Gazette* of Charleston," *South Carolina Historical and Genealogical Magazine* 44 (April 1943):85.

[2]Manuscript autobiography of Philip Phillips, 20-21, Phillips Family Papers, Manuscript Division, Library of Congress, Washington DC; "Schirmer Diary," *South Carolina Historical and Genealogical Magazine* 69 (January 1968):65.

[3]Phillips Autobiography, 21, and the Legal Files, Phillips Family Papers.

for another term. He and his family did, however, remain in Washington, where Philip returned to his legal practice.[4]

From 1855 to 1861 Phillips's practice before the United States Supreme Court "slowly but steadily increased." Among those who obviously had every confidence in Phillips as an attorney was Edwin M. Stanton, former attorney general of the United States. Besides working together on legal matters, Phillips and Stanton were close personal friends who often discussed the bitter sectional conflict between the North and South. Other influential friends of Phillips and his family included Associate Supreme Court Justice James M. Wayne and Reverdy Johnson, a prominent Maryland congressman.[5] Not so friendly with the Phillipses, but well known to them, was Secretary of State William H. Seward. At one time during their prewar stay in Washington, when they lived near the Patent Office, Seward was their neighbor. He and Eugenia frequently quarreled over the issues that were dividing the North and South.[6]

The firing on Fort Sumter, which dramatically announced the beginning of the Civil War, had occurred just four months before Federal agents on 24 August 1861, burst into the Phillips's home on I Street and declared all persons in the house under arrest. From top to bottom the house was searched, for the agents were convinced they would find evidence proving that the Phillipses were Confederate spies. Eugenia's family letters, which no doubt contained derogatory remarks about President Abraham Lincoln and the government, were in a box in the washstand. She managed to whisper to Phebe Dunlap, her "confidential maid," telling her to destroy the box. Eugenia trusted Phebe's "Irish shrewdness," and she was not disappointed; for on the pretext of being very thirsty

---

[4]William Garrett, *Reminiscences of Public Men in Alabama for Thirty Years* (Spartanburg SC, 1975) 405-407; Manuscript journal of the Alabama House of Representatives, 1851, Alabama State Archives, Montgomery; Phillips Autobiography, 24-30.

[5]Phillips Autobiography, 38; Edwin M. Stanton to Philip Phillips, 21 February 1861, Phillips Family Papers; Caroline Phillips Myers, "Memoirs of Events in 1861," Phillips-Myers Collection, Southern Historical Collection, University of North Carolina at Chapel Hill.

[6]Myers, "Memoirs."

and needing to leave for a drink of water, the maid, with the incriminating evidence tucked under her dress, got away from her guard long enough to burn the letters.[7]

The scene at the Phillips's home must have been the epitome of pandemonium. When Eugenia's daughter Fanny dropped a scrap of paper out of an upstairs window, it was picked up by a passing friend. Several of the distressed government agents went to great lengths to secure "this important document," as Eugenia sarcastically called it, only to find the words, "We are all arrested and treated with indignity." An unidentified woman visitor, who was a Roman Catholic, nervously crossed and recrossed herself and begged Eugenia to tell the agents that she had never sent any letters South and that she visited the Phillips's home only infrequently. The Phillipses were relieved when the distraught lady was released an hour or two later. Upon collecting all the family's correspondence that could be found, the agents departed, leaving soldiers to occupy the house and keep the Phillips family under house arrest.[8]

The occupation of the Phillipses' home lasted a week; but soon after the house was searched, Eugenia, two of her daughters, Fanny and Lina, and her sister, Martha Levy, were moved to the home of Rose Greenhow on 16th Street. Mrs. Greenhow was widely believed to be a Confederate spy and was also under arrest. Her house became the prison "where all the female Rebels could be better cared for," according to Eugenia Phillips. She described their situation at the Greenhow house: "So my two daughters, sister, and myself were thrust into two dirty, small attic rooms, evidently where negroes had lived, with no comforts of any kind. The stove (broken) served us for a table and washstand, while a punch bowl grew into a washbasin. Two filthy straw mattresses kept us warm, and Yankee soldiers were placed at our bedroom door to prevent our escape. Low men took charge of us, their conduct becoming so rude that one of the soldiers, filled with pity, wrote us a note while his watch came round, saying he would take a note to Mr. Phillips,

---

[7]Jacob R. Marcus, ed., "Eugenia Phillips, Defiant Rebel," *Memoirs of American Jews* (New York NY, 1974) 3:163-67; Phillips Autobiography, 42-43.

[8]Marcus, "Eugenia Phillips, Defiant Rebel," 3:166-67.

who had not been arrested but was at home with the younger children that night."[9]

While the women were confined, Philip Phillips worked hard through Reverdy Johnson, Edwin Stanton, and Judge James Wayne to obtain their release. In one of the messages she received from her husband during her incarceration, Eugenia heard that their old neighbor, Secretary of State Seward, whom Eugenia bitterly labeled that "arch hypocrite," was behind the imprisonment. At one point during her confinement, Eugenia was incensed to learn the newspapers had reported her release and removal to the South under a flag of truce.[10]

Finally, on 18 September, after more than three weeks of being under arrest, the Phillips women were released, largely because of the intervention of Philip Phillips's powerful friends, especially Stanton. Meanwhile, Phillips had arranged through Seward for permission to take his family from Washington and head southward. He sold everything except his law library, entrusting it to a friend, and prepared to leave. The departure from Washington was facilitated by General Winfield Scott, who permitted Phillips to carry with him $5,000 in gold and furnished the steamboat that took the family to Virginia. A ten-day stay in Richmond afforded Phillips an opportunity to report his impressions of the Northern frame of mind with regard to the war. His report that the North was determined to restore the Union at the cost of "the last man and the last dollar" was not what Southern leaders wished to hear. According to Caroline (or Lina) Phillips Myers's account, written a half century later, Eugenia carried a coded message from Rose Greenhow in a ball of yarn and delivered it to President Jefferson Davis of the Confederacy.[11] What the message said remains unknown.

From Richmond the Phillips family went ultimately to New Orleans where Philip opened a law office, only to find that "in time of war the laws are silent." Scarcity of legal business, as it turned out,

---

[9]Ibid., 167.

[10]Ibid., 168-74; Myers, "Memoirs."

[11]Jacob R. Marcus, ed., "Philip Phillips, Southern Unionist," *Memoirs of American Jews*, 3:152-53; Myers, "Memoirs."

was not his only problem. On 29 April 1862, Union forces com-
manded by General Benjamin F. Butler captured New Orleans.
Given the compulsion of his wife and daughters to express their
Southern sympathies so vocally, Phillips probably knew trouble
was not far away now. Only two months passed before Eugenia's
defiance brought the Phillipses to grief once more. On Saturday, 29
June 1862, a funeral procession for an officer in the Union army—
one Lieutenant DeKay—passed beneath the balcony of the Phillipses' home. As it passed, Eugenia, standing on the balcony, burst
into laughter and cheers. The next morning a soldier appeared at
the Phillipses' home and informed Eugenia that he was under orders to take her to General Butler. A wave of apprehension swept
over the family; but convinced that there must be some mistake,
Eugenia, accompanied by her husband, went with the soldier to the
customhouse where "the autocrat," as she caustically called Butler,
presided. She noted that Butler "styled himself Christ's vicere-
gent." When Philip Phillips was told that he could not go with his
wife into Butler's chamber, Eugenia sat down and defiantly announced that only by dragging her would they get her in there
alone. She won her point, as Butler relented and permitted Philip
to accompany his wife.[12]

The confrontation with Butler was brief, for Eugenia's presence
apparently made him seethe with anger. As she approached him,
he screamed that she had been observed "laughing and mocking at
a Federal officer," referring to her behavior on the balcony the day
before. When the general continued his verbal abuse, Philip interrupted him and said he would tolerate only the language of a
gentleman in the presence of his wife. At this Butler, "trembling
with rage," ordered Phillips from the room, but he refused to go.
Butler then slowly wrote out Special Order No. 150, which sen-
tenced Eugenia Phillips to Ship Island, Mississippi, an island in the
Gulf of Mexico, until further notice. Eugenia believed that Butler
took his time so that she would throw herself on his mercy, but her

---

[12]Marcus, "Eugenia Phillips, Defiant Rebel," 3:180-85; Myers, "Memoirs."

"holy indignation" led her to stand, with arms folded, and look on with "silent contempt."[13]

Special Order No. 150 was highly explicit. It noted that Eugenia Phillips had already been imprisoned in Washington for "traitorous proclivities and acts." She was accused of training her children to spit on United States officers, and it was noted that one of them had done so. She and her husband had apologized and had been forgiven, but now she had laughed and mocked during the funeral procession of Lieutenant DeKay, contemptuously giving as her explanation that she was in "good spirits" that day. Henceforth, she was to be regarded "as a uncommon, bad and dangerous woman, stirring up strife and inciting to riot," and would be confined to Ship Island "till further orders." Only one female servant would be allowed to accompany her. She was to live in a house assigned for hospital purposes and have a soldier's ration, which she would have to cook herself. No written or verbal communications were to be allowed with her except through General Butler's office.[14]

When Butler was finished, Eugenia Phillips was taken to an adjoining room and locked up for the night, while Philip Phillips made his way home to a "heartbroken family." On the second day of her imprisonment, she was told that a steamboat would take her to Ship Island the next day. Her family packed her things and her maid Phebe made preparations to accompany her. Eugenia's husband and sons went with them to the boat, as "old venerable men, and others" removed their hats and stood in silence as Eugenia passed by.[15]

The boat ride lasted thirty-six hours, during which time Eugenia and Phebe were subjected to "whisky drinking, ribald talk unfit for a female ear." Upon arriving at the island, Eugenia was in-

---

[13]Manuscript accounts of Eugenia Phillips's dealings with General Butler and her diary of the events of 1862 are in the Phillips-Myers Collection. The entry giving this particular information is dated 29 June 1862. Also see Marcus, "Eugenia Phillips, Defiant Rebel," 3:186-87.

[14]Newspaper clipping of Special Order No. 150, Phillips-Myers Collection.

[15]Marcus, "Eugenia Phillips, Defiant Rebel," 3:188-89; Diary of Eugenia Phillips, 1-3 July 1862, Phillips-Myers Collection.

formed that her quarters were not ready and that she would have to spend another day on the boat. Already in a "nervous state," she announced that another day on the boat would drive her crazy or kill her. An officer, called Lieutenant Blodgett in Eugenia's diary and Captain Blodgett in her memoirs years later, had pity on her, and had her and Phebe rowed ashore in a boat. In her memoirs, written after the war, Eugenia described her island prison: "Ship Island is a sand bar, formed from the workings of the water all around. Not a tree or blade of grass shades the eye or person from the fearful heat. Neither man nor beast . . . found the island inhabitable [sic]. Having walked about one-fourth of a mile, Capt. B. suddenly stopped, saying he wished to prepare me for my home. In a path before me stood a box, or small room, fixed upright on a hill of sand."[16]

What Eugenia Phillips called a box or small room was actually a railroad boxcar. There can be little doubt that she and her maid spent a miserable summer on Ship Island, but in spite of the discomfort they suffered from the heat and the insects, they tried to make the best of a grim situation. Eugenia's diary and the letters she wrote to her family reveal that her spirit remained defiant and her tongue sarcastic. She spoke sneeringly of General Neal Dow, commander of the forces on Ship Island, calling him a "Black Republican." And when another female prisoner named Mrs. LaRue was released on 4 August Eugenia asked her to tell General Butler when she reached New Orleans that Mrs. Phillips was still in "good spirits." According to Eugenia's later memoirs, Butler dispatched someone once a week to inquire about her health, hoping she would beg and plead to be released, but she never did. She urged Philip to ask no favors, for she preferred rotting on Ship Island to asking Butler for anything.[17]

With regard to Eugenia's living conditions on Ship Island, General Butler's directions were not carried out. As noted, her first shelter was a railroad boxcar, not a hospital house, and when she

---

[16]Marcus, "Eugenia Phillips, Defiant Rebel," 3:190-91; Diary of Eugenia Phillips, 3 July 1862.

[17]Marcus, "Eugenia Phillips, Defiant Rebel," 3:192-93; Diary of Eugenia Phillips, 3 July and 1, 6 August 1862.

was moved from the car, her new quarters turned out to be the former post office. Eugenia described it as looking much like a Southern barn that kept out neither wind nor rain. Mosquitoes and flies were so bad she reported that the mosquitoes established an early "curfew." She blessed the man who had invented the mosquito net.[18]

According to Butler's Special Order, Eugenia and Phebe were to cook their own food, a soldier's ration, but this did not work out in practice either. She recorded that at one point the cook took pity on them and attempted to make some bread they could eat; the bread they normally received was too hard to be eaten and could not be softened enough to make it edible. They thought, according to Eugenia, of trying to engage the services of a pile driver or of using steam to see if it could "penetrate the indomitable loaf." Besides hard bread, they had tongue one morning for breakfast and sardines the next; for dinner they had the same. The cook, whom Eugenia jokingly called "our chef de cuisine," would enter and announce, "Thar's you *brikfast* the best I could do." About the only comfort the women could take in their meals was that they were served in a pan that, from a distance, looked like silver. Therefore, they could imagine that the food was going to be of high quality.[19]

In addition to poor housing and almost inedible food, Eugenia found the inhabitants of Ship Island and their behavior quite distressing. She recorded in her diary that the island was the abode of "negroes, soldiers, contractors, sutlers, piddlars, black republicans, sailors, and Officers." Their manner of dress, especially officers walking about in their undershirts, offended her, and she complained that the air was "musical with curses and other elegancies of language." She was also bothered by the familiarity that existed between whites and blacks on the island, plus the constant arrival of runaway blacks whose coming brought a "jubilee of prayers, holy groans, and loud singing." Because she was a former

---

[18]Diary of Eugenia Phillips, 9 July 1862, and Eugenia Phillips to her friends and husband, 9 July 1862, Phillips-Myers Collection.

[19]Diary of Eugenia Phillips, 9 July 1862, and Eugenia Phillips to her "Darling Household," 17 July 1862, Phillips-Myers Collection.

slaveowner and a thoroughly Southern woman, this kind of behavior "aroused her indignation."[20]

To add to her misery, Eugenia at one point became ill during her confinement on Ship Island. Sometime between 9 and 20 August, she was so sick for a week that she could not lift her head without fainting. She experienced severe pain in her eyes and back, but the army doctor treated her "very skillfully," and Phebe never left her bedside. The illness no doubt broke her spirit a little, for she wrote Philip that she was no longer going to conceal from him all that she suffered. She became a little frightened in early September when a soldier died and the doctor reported that yellow fever might have been the cause. After Eugenia's illness and the yellow fever scare, Phebe's health broke down, and what Eugenia called her "chronic disease" began to worsen. Eugenia requested that Philip send someone else to her so that Phebe could go home.[21]

During those difficult, hot summer days Eugenia kept up her morale by reading such material as the *Deserted Village* and the *Vicar of Wakefield*, which she said she had read for the hundredth time. She also studied French to help pass the time. From her family she received loving letters and "creature comforts," which meant much to her. She was no doubt encouraged also by words of praise, such as those written to her by Amanda Levy, apparently a relative who lived in New Orleans. Amanda wrote, "Future historians will vie with each other for the honor of writing your biography." She also reported to Eugenia that pilgrimages two or three times a week to the Phillipses' home had become "quite the rage." Sympathy for her in New Orleans was "wide spread and real."[22]

While Eugenia was on Ship Island several false reports circulated, each claiming that she had been released, but it was not until three months had passed that she was finally permitted to leave her island prison. The exact date of her release and who was responsible for it are not known with certainty, although the evidence in-

---

[20]Diary of Eugenia Phillips, 9 July 1862.

[21]Eugenia Phillips to Philip Phillips, 20 August and 4 September 1862, Phillips-Myers Collection.

[22]Eugenia Phillips to her friends and husband, 9 July 1862; Eugenia Phillips to Fan and Flo [Phillips], 25 July 1862; Amanda Levy to Eugenia Phillips, 26 July 1862, Phillips-Myers Collection.

dicates that Reverdy Johnson had arranged it at the end of September. On 2 October she gave an account of her property to the provost marshal in New Orleans and admitted to being "an EN-EMY of the United States." Sometime after making this declaration she appeared unexpectedly at the Phillipses' home. Immediately there ensued a great emotional scene during which family members laughed and wept. Eugenia had kept control of her nerves as long as she could, and then the family's emotional outburst caused her to break down. She later described what happened: "My brain appeared on fire. My nerves lost all control, and I fell fainting and paralyzed on the floor. My screams were heard over the neighborhood. I lost all consciousness, and physicians were summoned. I was pronounced in a very critical condition, and to be kept perfectly quiet, else the consequences would be fatal."[23]

Since Philip Phillips and his wife had refused to take an oath of allegiance to the United States, it was hardly possible for the family to remain in New Orleans. Consequently, Philip secured a passport through the Federal lines from General George F. Shepley, and at the end of October 1862, the Phillips family and other refugees left New Orleans by boat. After spending some time in Mobile, Alabama, and Marietta, Georgia, Philip Phillips and his family settled down in LaGrange, Georgia, where they remained until after the war was over. There Eugenia Phillips took delight in "nursing the wounded and dying, alleviating in every way the desolation and misery which civil war surely brings."

By 1867 Philip Phillips was back in Washington, again practicing law. So successfully did he plead causes before the United States Supreme Court that he was eulogized in laudatory terms by important men upon his death in 1884. Eugenia, never forgetting what she went through in 1861 and 1862 because of her beliefs, lived to be eighty-one. She died in 1902.[24]

---

[23]Marcus, "Eugenia Phillips, Defiant Rebel," 3:194-95; Jacob C. Levy to Martha and Emma [Eugenia's sisters], 24 July 1862; E. Warren Moise to Mrs. Frederick Myers, 16 October 1862; and Provost Marshal's Receipt to Eugenia Levy Phillips, Phillips-Myers Collection.

[24]Marcus, "Eugenia Phillips, Defiant Rebel," 3:161, 195-96; Marcus, "Philip Phillips, Southern Unionist," 3:133, 154-60; "Biographical Information Contained in the Guide and Resolutions Made Upon the Death of Philip Phillips"; and E. Warren Moise to Mrs. Frederick Myers, 16 October 1862, Phillips Family Papers.

Surely many women suffered because of the Civil War. But Eugenia Phillips's experience is somewhat unique in that she was numbered among the very few women who were designated as "uncommon, bad, and dangerous." Actually she was, as her husband said, indiscreet but not dangerous. She refused to conceal her beliefs, and proudly proclaimed them in a belligerent manner. Looking back on her experience, one might not be able to endorse the cause that she so pugnaciously supported; but one can admire her courage and sympathize with her for suffering punishment that appears now to have been drastic and uncalled-for. She was twice a victim of overreaction by the Federal authorities. That she annoyed her enemies cannot be questioned; that she was dangerous to them is doubtful.

8

Philip Phillips,
Jurist and Statesman

by David T. Morgan

In the spring of 1807 Aaron Phillips, a German Jew who resided in Georgetown, South Carolina, went to Charleston and there married Caroline Lazarus, daughter of Marks Lazarus, a Revolutionary War veteran and prominent member of the Charleston Jewish community.[1] Nine months later, on 13 or 17 December (the date is in dispute), Caroline Lazarus Phillips bore Aaron their first child—Philip Phillips.[2]

As a boy, Phillips attended the best schools in Charleston, including one conducted by the controversial Isaac Harby, instructor

---

[1]Barnett Abraham Elzas, comp., *Jewish Marriage Notices from the Newspaper Press of Charleston, S.C., 1775-1906* (New York NY, 1917), 26 March, 1807; Barnett Abraham Elzas, *The Old Jewish Cemeteries at Charleston, S.C., A Transcript of the Inscriptions of Their Tombstones, 1762-1903* (Charleston SC, 1903) 68; Philip Phillips Autobiography, Phillips Family Papers, Library of Congress, Manuscript Division, Washington DC, 1; Phillips-Myers Collections, Southern Historical Collection, Louis Round Wilson Library, University of North Carolina at Chapel Hill, from information about the Phillips and Myers families in the introductory material.

[2]The date of Philip Phillips's birth is somewhat questionable. Authorities say 13 December 1807, but in his autobiography (manuscript), Philip Phillips notes it as 17 December 1807. See Phillips Autobiography, 1.

at the College of Charleston, newspaper editor and publisher, playwright, internationally known drama critic, and a pioneer reformer of Judaism.[3] The young Phillips probably acquired a considerable amount of intellectual curiosity from his dynamic teacher during the several years he boarded at Harby's school; but when, at age fifteen, he went away to a military academy in Connecticut, he apparently fell in line with that school's emphasis on physical training and began to neglect his studies. In later years, Phillips reflected on his three years at the academy and regretted his failure to be more studious. He did not regret, however, attending the academy, for he was convinced that the rigorous physical training he received there had contributed significantly to the good health he enjoyed on into his sixties.[4]

At age eighteen, Phillips returned to Charleston and decided upon a career in law. He entered the law office of John Gadsden, United States district attorney in Charleston and a member of one of South Carolina's most prominent families. From this highly esteemed and successful Charleston lawyer, Phillips learned the legal profession. Three years later the young Jewish lawyer, now twenty-two years of age, was admitted to the South Carolina bar, a feat achieved by only sixteen Jews between 1824 and 1860.[5]

During the years he was training for a legal career, Phillips, along with his father, became involved in Isaac Harby's struggle to reform the practice of Judaism in Charleston's Congregation Beth Elohim. Reacting against the rigid synagogue procedures that Beth Elohim had patterned after the Bevis Marks Congregation of London, Harby and forty-six of his followers requested a shorter service incorporating the use of the English language and including a sermon. When the petition was tabled, a group organized the Reformed Society of Israelites. Although the society had fifty members by 1826, and announced its intention of building a synagogue

---

[3]*The Isaac Harby Prayer Book* (Charleston SC, 1974) preface.

[4]Phillips Autobiography, 1-3.

[5]Barnett Abraham Elzas, *The Jews of South Carolina* (Philadelphia PA, 1905) 205-206; John Belton O'Neall, *Biographical Sketches of the Bench and Bar of South Carolina*, 2 vols. (Charleston SC, 1859) 2: 51-55; Phillips Autobiography, 6-7.

as soon as enough money could be raised, it did not continue to flourish. Harby, for economic reasons, left Charleston, as did other of the Reformers. By 1833, the Reformed Society was on the wane; the panic of 1837 ended its life. Aaron Phillips served as the society's president in 1825, and Philip Phillips as its secretary in 1828. Perhaps the failure of the society to achieve its objectives left the younger Phillips disenchanted with religion, since all the evidence suggests that he abandoned the practice of Judaism almost completely.[6]

Sometime in 1828 Philip Phillips left Charleston and moved to Cheraw, South Carolina, where he began a law practice and lived with his "bachelor uncle." When the uncle decided to marry, Phillips took up residence in "the hotel kept by Mr. Steinmetz." Among the hotel's attractions were low rates and the two pretty daughters of the proprietor. Within a short time Phillips became a circuit-riding lawyer and earned enough money to live, as he put it, "without embarrassment."[7]

While living in Cheraw, Phillips became seriously interested in politics, largely because the issue of nullification had polarized the views of South Carolinians and prompted all concerned men to take a definite stand. The young Jewish lawyer took his stand with the Union Democrats, or the Union and States' Rights party. Before long Phillips became a leader of the Union forces, reflected by his selection as chairman of the party in the Chesterfield District.[8] Acting in this capacity, he wrote state Senator Christopher Butler Pegues, who represented the Chesterfield District, and asked him to vote against both nullification and the calling of a convention to discuss the issue. A negative vote on these two matters, Phillips contended, was what a majority in the district wanted. Pegues replied that he would always defer to the sentiment of a majority of his con-

---

[6]Elzas, *Jews of South Carolina*, 147-65; *Harby Prayer Book*, preface; Bertram Wallace Korn, *The Jews of Mobile, 1763-1841* (Cincinnati OH, 1970) 46; Harry Simonhoff, *Saga of American Jewry, 1865-1914* (New York NY, 1959) 20.

[7]Phillips Autobiography, 6-7.

[8]C[hristopher] B[utler] Pegues to Philip Phillips, 26 October 1832, Phillips Family Papers; Emily Bellinger Reynolds and Joan Reynolds Fount, *Biographical Directory of the Senate of the State of South Carolina, 1776-1964* (Columbia SC, 1964) 228.

stituents, but in this case he had grave doubts that the Union party convention in the district represented a majority. In fact, claimed Pegues, the information that had reached him suggested that the meeting of the Union Democrats was very small, having no more than forty people in attendance. Moreover, he had received another request from a much larger group to vote the other way. Certain that Phillips did not speak for a majority in the district, Senator Pegues clearly stated that he would use his own discretion in casting his vote.[9]

Meanwhile, Phillips had kept in touch with James Blair, a Union Democrat who represented the South Carolina counties of Kershaw, Lancaster, Chesterfield, and Sumter in the United States House of Representatives. In the summer of 1832, Blair informed Phillips that he had voted for the Tariff of 1832, but that the Nullifiers had voted against it and had induced several other "hot-blooded Southrons," who were not Nullifiers, to join them in their negative vote. To Blair, all Nullifiers were would-be destroyers of not only the tariff system, but the whole federal government as well. The Union party congressman obviously held Phillips in high esteem, since he encouraged him to plunge more deeply into politics by offering himself as a candidate for some important political office. Blair also took Phillips into his confidence by discussing with him the matter of Martin Van Buren's candidacy for the vice-presidency of the United States. Although Blair did not like Van Buren and had voted for James Barbour of Virginia at the national Democratic convention in Baltimore, he still urged Jackson's election and encouraged Phillips to ignore the vice-presidential candidate, Van Buren, and work for the election of Jackson. Finally, Blair admonished Phillips to keep fighting the "heresy" of nullification in the Chesterfield District.[10]

Phillips did indeed continue the fight. When the state legislature, packed with Nullifiers, passed a law designed to place control of the state militia in the hands of the Nullifiers, Phillips, at the urging of friends, ran for the colonelcy of the Chesterfield regiment

---

[9]Pegues to Phillips, 26 October 1832, Phillips Family Papers.

[10]James Blair to Philip Phillips, 2 July 1832, Phillips Family Papers.

and won. Later in life he confessed that he had had little taste and less capacity for the post; his purpose was to test the new militia law in the courts. As it turned out, a Union man in Lancaster District had acted before Phillips, with the result that the law was declared unconstitutional.[11]

Among the delegates to the Nullification Convention in 1832 were Phillips and three other Jews—Chapman Levy, Philip Cohen, and Myer Jacobs. Levy joined Phillips in voting against nullification, while Cohen and Jacobs voted with the majority for it.[12] When Henry Clay's Compromise Tariff of 1833 was passed by the United States Congress and signed by President Jackson, South Carolina's Governor Robert Y. Hayne was persuaded to call another convention. This second convention, in an atmosphere of controversy, rescinded the 1832 Ordinance of Nullification. According to Phillips, the Union party minority in the second convention numbered no more than thirty delegates, but it was a "determined minority" that fought valiantly against the Nullifiers. Phillips, though only twenty-five years old and the youngest delegate present, showed no reluctance in taking a very active part in the proceedings.[13]

When the thirty-first General Assembly met in 1834, Philip Phillips was there as a member of the South Carolina House of Representatives. Tension still ran high between the Union men and the Nullifiers. An effort was made to discredit the Union Democrats and presumably to unseat them. Fortunately, men of good will on both sides worked out a compromise to restore peace, if not harmony, between the two factions. The key figures in arranging the compromise were former Governor James A. Hamilton for the Nullifiers and Philip Phillips for the Union Democrats.[14]

In April of 1834 James Blair suddenly died. This left the South Carolina Union Democrats with no voice in the United States Congress. Blair's seat was up for grabs, and both the Unionists and the

---

[11]Phillips Autobiography, 7-11.

[12]Ibid.; Charles Reznikoff and Uriah Z. Engleman, *The Jews of Charleston* (Philadelphia PA, 1950) 100-201.

[13]Phillips Autobiography, 11-12.

[14]Ibid., 15-17.

Nullifiers attached the utmost significance to winning it. The Nullifiers wanted it so that the state's congressional delegation could offer a united front against the Jackson administration. The Unionists wanted it to prove to the rest of the nation that not all South Carolinians had committed themselves to the treasonous doctrine of nullification. As far as the Unionists were concerned, they, not the Nullifiers, were champions of liberty, and the state laws passed to implement nullification were nothing short of treasonable acts. Consequently, the Unionists worked hard to suppress local jealousies and to unite on a single candidate. The bitterly contested special congressional election was held in June 1834. In spite of some alleged political trickery and corruption, former Governor Richard I. Manning, candidate of the Union Democrats, defeated the candidate of the Nullifiers by the narrow margin of 600 votes. Phillips's Chesterfield District, which some of the Unionist leaders had regarded as a source of grave doubt and concern, gave Manning a majority of 250 votes. Various letters written by Unionist leaders during the campaign make it clear that while Phillips had originally favored the candidacy of Judge Daniel Huger, he supported Manning and helped him win the election.[15]

While serving in the second session of the thirty-first General Assembly, Phillips decided, at the suggestion of Colonel Thomas Williams of the York District, to move to Mobile, Alabama. Once in Mobile, Phillips and Williams formed a law partnership, but it lasted for only a short while. Even so, Phillips made Mobile his home for the next eighteen years. He became a very successful attorney, earning about $8,000 per year, which, he said, was easily made and "still more easily expended." His legal practice brought Phillips into close association with some prominent Alabamians, such as Edmund S. Dargan, who later became chief justice of the Alabama Supreme Court, and Governor John Nayle. Among other things, Phillips became the attorney of the Bank of Mobile for a retainer of $2,000 per year.[16]

---

[15]James Chestnut to Phillips, 11 April, 21 May, and 6 June 1834; Daniel E. Huger to Phillips, 20 April, 1834; Richard I. Manning to Phillips, 8 June 1834; John P. Richardson to Phillips, 25 April, 18 May, and 3 September 1834; Neal Vaughn to Phillips, 22 May 1834, Phillips Family Papers.

[16]Phillips Autobiography, 19-22.

In 1836 Phillips returned to Charleston and married sixteen-year-old Eugenia Levy. The wedding took place on 7 September 1836.[17] Not long afterward, the newlyweds left for Mobile. They rode the 136 miles by train from Charleston to Hamburg. From there, they took the stagecoach to Montgomery, Alabama, a journey that lasted seven days and nights and took them "over some very rough and hilly country in Georgia." In Montgomery, the couple boarded a "little steamer, called the 'Fox' " and started down the Alabama River to Mobile—another seven-day journey. The river, according to Phillips, was beautiful to behold with its green banks studded with flowers, its blue water, and its large flocks of twittering parakeets.[18] In view of the fact that Phillips was observing the river through a honeymooner's eyes, it is entirely possible that the river appeared more beautiful to him than it might have to other observers.

Just as Philip Phillips had been a political activist in South Carolina, so was he in Alabama. He spoke out on all political issues; as he put it, he "harangued the people" in nearly every "corner of the city" of Mobile. In 1844 he was elected to the Alabama legislature and served as chairman of the federal relations committee.[19] Although Phillips was apparently not an imposing figure in the work of the legislature during this, his first term, he was a positive force, making a strong effort to push through a bill requiring a "thorough geological survey of the state." Phillips believed that Alabamians needed to have some accurate idea of the state's wealth in minerals. The bill was recommended to the house by a committee, but the representatives, in no mood to appropriate the necessary funds, refused to pass the bill.[20]

Phillips did not let this setback dampen his enthusiasm, for he remained an apostle of progress for Alabama. Five years after he

---

[17]"The Schirmer Diary," *South Carolina Historical and Genealogical Magazine* 69 (January 1968): 65.

[18]Phillips Autobiography, 21.

[19]William Garrett, *Reminiscences of Public Men in Alabama for Thirty Years* (Spartanburg SC, 1975) 376; Phillips Autobiography, 21.

[20]Phillips Autobiography, 21; "A Speech delivered by Philip Phillips, President of the Railroad Convention held at Talladega, Alabama, September, 1849," 17.

first represented Mobile in the Alabama house, he was elected president of the Railroad or Internal Improvement Convention that met at Talladega in September 1849. To the convention representatives he delivered an eloquent and enlightened speech on Alabama's economic situation. He pointed out that, economically speaking, there were really two Alabamas. North Alabama used the Tennessee and Mississippi rivers and shipped goods to market by way of New Orleans, while south Alabama traded through Mobile. He urged the connection of the two sections by means of railroad, proposing a line that would run from Gunter's Landing to Selma. His proposed route was drawn to carry the train through those Alabama counties that were rich in minerals.

The day would come, Phillips predicted, when Alabama would realize much more wealth from coal, iron, marble, and limestone than from cotton. All kinds of goods, including highly marketable coal and iron, could be shipped by railroad to Selma and from there by river to Mobile, Phillips asserted. He argued that the system he proposed would enable Alabama's northern counties to ship cheaper and faster than the system that they had used traditionally. Phillips vigorously challenged the widely held notion that Alabama was too poor to build a railroad. He was firmly convinced that because Alabama was one of the top cotton-producing states, the resources for building the proposed transportation system were available. He closed his speech by urging the convention to have faith that the railroad could be built and to show "its faith in works."[21]

By this time Phillips had made a name for himself as a jurist as well as a political leader. In 1840 he "prepared and published a digest" of all decisions that had been rendered by the Alabama Supreme Court. Six years later he came out with a revised edition. Phillips claimed that his digest was the first work of its kind. Perhaps it was the publicity the digest brought him that prompted the Alabama legislature to elect him judge of the Criminal Court in Mobile. On 24 February 1846, Governor Joshua L. Martin, pursuant to the action taken by the legislature, appointed Phillips to that judge-

---

[21]Speech to the Railroad Convention, 1-20.

ship. Although he accepted the job, Phillips soon resigned from it on the ground that it severely restricted his legal practice.[22]

As Phillips's reputation as a jurist spread, his influence as a political leader increased also. By 1850 he had become very friendly with William R. King, one of Alabama's United States senators and a leading Democrat at both the state and national levels. One of King's letters to Phillips makes it clear that the senator considered the Mobile lawyer a key figure in the Alabama Democratic party. King was deeply concerned about party divisions that might pave the way of the Whigs to power in the state. He obviously believed that Phillips could play a major part in restoring Democratic harmony.[23]

When the Alabama legislature met in 1851, Phillips was a member, returning for the first time since 1844. This time, as chairman of the committee on internal improvement, he was one of the most active members of the house. He was also a member of the committee on the judiciary; and a perusal of the house's journal for the session reveals that he introduced numerous bills and motions. His most impressive work, however, was done in committee. As chairman of the committee on internal improvement, he wrote a significant report that was presented to the house. The report demonstrated that the legislature had "never expended one dollar of its own treasure for the advancement of any great work of improvement." Phillips lamented in his report that Alabama's "destiny seems to be to grow old and poor together." The only way to prosperity, he contended, was through a system of internal improvements that would give Alabamians ready access to markets. A bill that called for spending $230,000 from funds "donated by the General Government [federal government]" in order to start such a system was proposed in the report. Phillips offered detailed information on federal funds—information he had obtained with the

[22]Official commission from Joshua L. Martin to Philip Phillips, 24 February 1846, Phillips Family Papers; In the autobiography, Phillips states that he received the commission from Governor Benjamin Fitzpatrick, but apparently his memory was impaired, perhaps by old age.

[23]Phillips to William R. King, 1 June 1850 (copy); King to Phillips, 11 March 1851, Phillips Family Papers.

help of William R. King. The report was highly acclaimed, and 500
copies of it were printed by order of the legislature, but instead of
passing the comprehensive internal improvements plan that Phillips advocated, the legislators decided in favor of a piecemeal, less
effective approach. For example, several railroads that served only
a few localities were chartered, but none of them united northern
and southern Alabama as Phillips wanted the railroads to do.[24]

As chairman of a special committee on the Alabama legal code,
Phillips made another important legislative report. That extensive
report—the longest by far contained in the house's journal for
1851—presented a thorough analysis of the entire state legal code.
By order of the House, 2,500 copies of the report were printed.[25]

Phillips's impressive efforts in the legislature were merely a
prelude to weightier responsibilities and more personal recognition. He was easily the dominant figure at the state Democratic
convention in 1851. In June of 1852, he attended the national convention in Baltimore, where he had a part in the nomination of
Franklin Pierce as the Democratic candidate for president of the
United States. Later that month when William B. King, Pierce's
vice-presidential running mate, was attacked in the *Charleston Mercury*, Phillips won King's gratitude by rebutting the allegations and
criticism. In a letter of thanks to Phillips, King exuded confidence,
contending that the Democrats would win the presidential election
because they would carry the two key states of New York and
Ohio.[26]

Many men would have been delighted with opportunities to
mix with the national leaders of their party and would have sought
even more recognition, but the evidence strongly suggests that
Phillips shied away from this kind of activity. As a matter of fact,

---

[24]Garrett, *Reminiscences*, 406-407; manuscript journal of the Alabama House of
Representatives, 1851, Alabama Archives, Montgomery, Alabama; King to Phillips, 10 December, 1851, Phillips Family Papers. There is a copy of Phillips's
printed report in the Phillips Family Papers and a printed copy attached at the appropriate place in the Alabama House Journal, 1851.

[25]Alabama House Journal, 1851.

[26]Garrett, *Reminiscences*, 406; Phillips Autobiography, 24; King to Phillips, 26
June 1852, Phillips Family Papers.

when the Democratic convention of the Mobile District met in 1853 to nominate a candidate for Congress, Phillips, in characteristic fashion, was not even present. The convention, presided over by William R. Hallett, president of the Bank of Mobile and Phillips's longtime friend, could not decide on a candidate from among those seeking the nomination and so it turned unanimously to Phillips. When he was intercepted on his way to dinner and informed of the convention's action, Phillips reluctantly accepted the nomination. Subsequently, in a hard-fought campaign against Elihu Lockwood, the Whig candidate, Phillips was elected to the United States House of Representatives by a few hundred votes. On 24 November 1853, Governor Henry W. Collier signed Phillips's commission to the 33rd Congress.[27]

The Phillips family was soon off to Washington, and the new representative from the Mobile District showed no hesitation in assuming the same kind of active role that had characterized his efforts in the Alabama legislature two years earlier. He spoke out forthrightly on a number of minor issues such as the process by which an assistant secretary of the treasury should be appointed, the treaty-making powers of the president in the Gadsden Purchase, and the obligations of the United States government in the settlement of the French spoliation claims. He also played an important part in designing the famous and controversial Kansas-Nebraska bill. As a member of the House Committee on Territories, Phillips urged the bill's sponsor, Senator Stephen A. Douglas, to include in the provisions a statement *explicitly*, not implicitly, repealing the Missouri Compromise. Key members of the Senate and the House, including Phillips, conferred with President Franklin Pierce. The result of that conference was the acceptance of Phillips's position (a commonly held one among Southerners) based on the principle of congressional nonintervention with regard to slavery in the territories. It was agreed that the question of slavery in all states and territories should be left to the people who lived in them. Phillips was "activated" by what he believed was a "theoretical right." Looking back on the Kansas-Nebraska Act years later,

---

[27]Garrett, *Reminiscences*, 406-407; Phillips Autobiography, 25-26; commission from Governor Henry W. Collier to Philip Phillips, 24 November 1853.

Phillips recognized that it had "increased the slavery agitation and hastened the crisis of 1861." The tone of the statements indicates that he regretted his part in it. For in spite of his Southern ways, Phillips never gave up his commitment to the Union.[28]

During his days in Congress Phillips remained deeply involved in public issues. For instance, in the summer of 1855, when the anti-Catholic hysteria spawned by the Know-Nothing party resulted in demonstrations in Philadelphia, Pennsylvania, and Montgomery, Alabama, he took a forthright public stand against religious bigotry. Asserting that the Constitution of the United States had decreed "eternal divorce between civil and ecclesiastical jurisdiction," Phillips condemned the Know-Nothings as scum thrown off by the Democratic and Whig parties. People seeking office, he contended, should be judged by their "honesty and capability," not their religious faith. As far as he was concerned, the Know-Nothing movement, with its religious bigotry, was nothing less than an attack upon the Constitution.[29]

Because of this stand and others, Phillips enjoyed a national reputation by the time his term was up in Conress. So impressively did he conduct himself while he was in Washington that he was mentioned in many quarters as a potential secretary of the navy, but that appointment never came his way. He was renominated for a second term in Congress, but he declined to run again, claiming that he could not afford to serve on the salary that was provided him. He did, however, believe that Washington, D.C., offered greater opportunities to a man of his talents than did Mobile, and he resolved to move his residence and legal practice to the nation's capital.[30]

Philip Phillips became one of the most respected and successful attorneys to practice before the United States Supreme Court.

---

[28]Phillips Autobiography, 30; extract of notes of Philip Phillips; speech on the French spoliation bill; speech on the Mexican treaty bill; speech on the bill prescribing the manner of appointing the assistant secretary of the treasury; speech on the territorial bill.

[29]Letter on the religious proscription of Catholics, 4 July 1855, Phillips Family Papers.

[30]Garrett, *Reminiscences*, 406-407; Phillips Autobiography, 35.

When he died in 1884, some of the most prominent members of that bar eulogized him as "a jurist and statesman of rare ability" and as a man of "pure and exalted character."[31] Phillips's record reveals that he was no ordinary man. He was held in esteem by many in high places—people who were firsthand observers of his distinguished career. With that in mind one might ask: Was Phillips a great jurist and statesman? How can a perusal of his record produce anything but a strongly affirmative answer? If this is so, why has he fallen into obscurity, and why did he not climb to even greater heights than he did? The fact that he was never a cabinet member, supreme court justice, or even a longtime member of Congress probably accounts for his obscurity, since very few lawyers and one-term congressmen catch the eye of historians. But the question persists, why didn't he win a higher place in the national government?

This is the real question, one that is hard to answer, and which cries out for a plausible explanation. One writer, Harry Simonhoff, contends that, given Phillips's Unionist sentiments, he would have had a golden opportunity to become the Judah P. Benjamin of the North, but it never happened because of his flamboyant wife's pro-Southern views and various controversial encounters with the Union authorities.[32] This is an interesting idea, but it suggests no explanation of why Phillips missed his "destiny" *before* the Civil War. The ideal time for Phillips to have obtained an appointment to the cabinet was during the Buchanan administration, for his record in Congress was almost certainly pleasing to the president who sympathized with Southern views. There is another answer that seems more likely: Phillips fell victim to the Jacksonian democracy of which he was an adherent throughout his political career. He never gained a popular following because he did not have the personality of a charismatic politician. In his political views he was a Democrat, but in his personal ways, which included an aloofness from the masses, he was a Whig. William Garrett, Alabama's secretary of state for many years, first met Phillips in 1838. Years later

---

[31] Resolutions made on the death of Philip Phillips, Phillips Family Papers.

[32] Simonhoff, *Saga of American Jewry*, 20.

---

he described the Mobile attorney as a man whose personal appearance was "commanding and dignified" and as a "strong debater" and dedicated public servant. Even though Garrett considered Phillips "affable and courteous," he noted that he cared "very little for social enjoyments."[33] Phillips himself noted that during his campaign for Congress against Elihu Lockwood, he was accused of being "an enemy of the poor man." On another occasion, he was blasted in the newspapers for being an able but egotistical man.[34]

Whether or not Phillips distrusted the masses, the evidence indicates that he had an Olympian air about him that kept him from gaining and holding a wide political following. With the coming of Jacksonian democracy it was generally agreed that a person receiving an appointment to the president's cabinet should have ability, but it was imperative that he be able to make a political contribution. Phillips could not make that kind of contribution. If he had appeared on the American political scene a half-century earlier, before democracy came into its own, his name might well occupy a more prominent place alongside some of our early national leaders.

---

[33]Garrett, *Reminiscences*, 405-406.

[34]Phillips Autobiography, 26-28, 36-37.

9

Ludwig Lewisohn:
Up the Literary Stream
from Charleston and Beyond

by Daniel Walden

Ludwig Lewisohn was born in Berlin, 30 May 1883. At the age of four his grandmother taught him to read, and what he called his "real life" began.[1] Brought up in an assimilated German-Jewish family who were "Germans first and Jews afterwards," he knew that he was Jewish, but he was more excited by the unveiling of a Christmas tree. On an early visit to a synagogue on Yom Kippur, he remembered how impressed he was, but also how alien and strange he felt.[2] To his parents, Jacques and Minna, it was a foregone conclusion that a liberal education was the necessary foundation of right and noble living for Ludwig. His mother pinned all her hopes and love on her only son. From her and his grandmother he got his penchant for scholarship; from his mother, who sang German songs to him, he got his sensitivity for music.[3]

---

[1]Ludwig Lewisohn, *Up Stream* (New York NY, 1926) 21. The book was originally published by Boni and Liveright in 1922.

[2]Ibid., 12-13.

[3]Ibid., 16.

Sometime in 1889, Jacques Lewisohn decided that the family had to emigrate to America. Having invested his inheritance unwisely, it seemed the only way out for him. Providentially, he had just received a letter from Siegfried Eloesser, Minna's younger brother, who gave the impression that he had been doing moderately well in South Carolina. When the Lewisohns arrived in St. Matthews, South Carolina, in 1890, they found a "squalid village" in which Siegfried was barely making a living, and Siegfried's wife, Fannie, in the eyes of her in-laws seemed an objectionable person. Ludwig recalled that she was "a Jewess of the Eastern European tradition, narrowminded, given over to the clattering ritual of pots and pans—'meaty and milky'—and very ignorant."[4] This was the reaction, despite the fact that the Lewisohns were impoverished gentility from Berlin, while Fannie had been brought up in Charleston. After another disastrous business venture, the Lewisohns had to move to Charleston. Having left the clean, orderly life of Berlin, they arrived in a small town where burly Negroes gabbled and white men whittled and spat tobacco. Ludwig's father was singled out because, when he was asked to affirm categorically his belief in a personal God by his Gentile neighbors, he smiled and hesitated.[5] Not being a "real Jew" was something that the local gentry could not accept.

In Charleston, Ludwig found a city of "sharp, rustling palmettoes, the splash and murmur of the incoming tide, the melancholy song of Negroes across the bay."[6] Having already been acculturated in St. Matthews, where he had attended a Methodist Sunday school and had begun to accept "the gospel story and the obvious implications of Pauline Christianity without question," he readily submerged himself in the new culture.[7] "If ever the child of an immigrant embraced the faith of the folk among whom it came," he

---

[4]Ibid., 41; see also Stanley Chyet, "Ludwig Lewisohn, The Years of Becoming," *American Jewish Archives* (October 1959): 126.

[5]*Up Stream*, 43.

[6]Ibid., 59.

[7]Ibid., 53.

wrote, "I was that child."[8] At the same time, it was unfortunate that Jacques and Minna looked down on the "North German peasants turned grocers," and the "ignorant semi-orthodox Jews from Posen" who made up a substantial part of Charleston's Jewish community.[9] Lacking any Jewish reinforcement, cultural or otherwise, and shunned by Charleston, Ludwig turned inward. The strain of melancholy, "the badge of all our tribe," as he put it much later, was deepened, and early he became aware of "our homelessness . . . of our terrible hopelessness" in the universe.[10] Uncertain of his relation to the Jewish group in Charleston and what should have been his primary associative group, and uncertain of his relationship to the Gentiles to whom he was drawn, he had to pay the price: an increase in tension, conflict, and inner pressure. At this point in his life he did not share what Kurt Lewin described as the one indispensable element constituting a group, "interdependence of fate," with the Jews.[11]

The more Lewisohn turned inward, the more he turned to books and to his mother, with whom he took long walks. Absorbed in reading Sir Walter Scott's Waverly novels, he forgot the duties and compulsions of the world. He also read Addison, Byron, and Dickens, and built the foundations of a sound and permanent knowledge of Latin and French, as well as the English poets. When he met anti-Semitism he excused it as a vagary of life, the exception to be tolerated. Actually, anti-Semitism helped encourage him to forget his German-Jewish past. By 1897 he felt himself to be an American, a Southerner, and a Christian. He abandoned the German books of earlier years, and even stopped speaking German at home.[12] Meanwhile, his growing inner turmoil resulted in a less active Methodism, and a brief attachment to Catholicism. "Oh, to cast

---

[8]Ibid., 53-54.

[9]Ibid., 62.

[10]Ibid., 68.

[11]Miriam Lewis Papenek, "Psychological Aspects of Minority Group Membership: The Concepts of Kurt Lewin," *Jewish Social Studies* 36 (January 1974): 77; Kurt Lewin, *Resolving Group Conflicts* (New York NY, 1948).

[12]*Up Stream*, 85, 76.

off one's burdens here at the foot of the Cross," he thought, "to solve, by one glorious acceptance, all the difficulties of life; to lay down all sins, all yearnings, all fears, all uncertainties; to be up-borne by the Eternal Strength; to rest in the love and boundless compassion of the Everlasting Arms!"[13]

At high school in Charleston, which Ludwig entered at age ten as a result of his mother's tutelage, he was influenced by Virgil C. Dibble, the headmaster, and by Thomas Della Torre, his Latin teacher, who "might have been a friend of Petronius . . . [or] a friend of Addison." It was Della Torre who recognized Lewisohn's talents for literature. It was in literature that Lewisohn lived; im-mersing himself in books helped him to escape from the sorrows and pains of the world around him. Paradoxically, though he sensed the difficulties a "German Jew" might have, he pushed himself deeper and deeper into the world of British literature, with its "alien culture and its alien code" so conducive, he thought, to his well-being. At his high school graduation he read his transla-tion of Horace's "Diffugere Nives." He considered himself a "gentleman" who believed in the South, Christianity, and the Democratic party, and agreed with the local view of Jews as "the intolerable tyranny of a barbarous and inferior race." All the while he was reading widely in Swift, Dryden, Pope, Addison, Johnson, and Goldsmith. In his then misanthropic state, Lewisohn felt at home with "the stark gloom of the great Dean [Swift] and the gen-tler melancholy of Johnson."[14]

From 1897 to 1901, Lewisohn attended the College of Charleston and graduated with two degrees, a bachelor's and a master's. His master's thesis was on Matthew Arnold. Passionately Anglo-Amer-ican, he was seen as a little German boy who looked very Jewish. Wanting to be accepted as a Southerner, he was hurt by the slights of his teachers and his classmates. As he wrote much later of Lan-celot Minor Harris, a Virginia aristocrat who was his English pro-fessor, he "never, I think, quite forgave me for being what I am." As a result, he recalled, "I withdrew into myself, with sullen pride

---

[13]Lewisohn, *The Broken Snare* (New York NY, 1908) 147-48, 208-10.

[14]*Up Stream*, ch. 4: "The Making of an Anglo-American."

and intensified ambition, convinced that [all anti-Semitic incidents were] local, exceptional, unrepresentative, and un-American."[15]

Probably to compensate for his feeling of frustration he devoted himself to his chosen calling, English literature. Believing that Matthew Arnold was "the clearest-souled Englishman of his century," he declared that the literary critic's tool was to seek truth in literature, as Arnold had done. Valuing Arnold's intellect and restraint, he described the Englishman's "control of the emotions of the intellect," while he stated that Arnold is "our poet, his struggle is our struggle, his victory is our victory." As he wrote of Arnold's struggles, Ludwig was undoubtedly aware of how close this was to his own struggles.[16]

During the next year, Lewisohn wrote a 50,000-word history of South Carolina literature. Published in the Charleston *News and Courier* in 1903 as "Books We Have Made," it was an essay in biography and criticism in which Lewisohn laid claim to a relationship with the South that was as remarkable for its scholarship as for its honesty and zeal. Attempting to correct the neglectful attitudes then prevalent toward early American literature, he was critical of the New England Puritan tradition. At the same time, he asserted that South Carolina, perhaps more than any other province, shared the literary atmosphere of the mother country. He also noted, honestly, that "the earlier literature of Carolina has not infrequently all sorts of respectable qualities, but is, alas, thoroughly unreadable."

Driven by his desire to see South Carolina through rose-colored glasses and by his critic's impulse to be objective, he described much of the literature of the Old South as provincial even as he called Henry Timrod, William Gilmore Simms, and Paul Hamilton Hayne "lasting additions" to American literature. Unfortunately, Ludwig's Southern chauvinism often got in the way. He so admired Simms's *War Poetry of the South*, for example, that he wrote that "it's a book in the face of which it is hard to stick to one's

---

[15]Ibid., 93, 101.

[16]Lewisohn, "A Study of Matthew Arnold," *Sewanee Review* 9 (October 1901): 442-56; 10 (April 1902): 143-59; 10 (July 1902): 302-19.

hardly acquired critical standards."[17] It seems that in noting how
Simms had been excluded by certain people, Ludwig felt more
keenly his own discrimination. As he defended Simms, he defended himself. As Carl Van Doren has written, Simms "suffered
from the conflict in him between his nature and the tradition which
he inherited."[18] In the same way, Ludwig suffered from the conflict
between his past and his desire to be a Southerner, a Christian, and
an American.

In 1903 Ludwig entered Columbia University. Reading books
that changed the whole tenor of his inner life, by Nietzsche, Haupt-
mann, Hoffmannsthal, Mann, and others, he found a new sentiment "grown inevitably from the sweat and tears, the yearning and
the aspiration of our mortal fate . . . [but] never set down because
it was a correct sentiment to which human nature must be made to
conform." When he received his second master's degree in 1904,
and was asked by Professor William P. Trent, one of his professors,
to write an introduction to an edition of Crevecoeur's *Letters from an
American Farmer*, he felt assured of his future. When he received
neither a further job offer nor even a recommendation, he asked
why. "A recent experience has shown me," wrote Professor Carpenter to Lewisohn, "how terribly hard it is for a man of Jewish
birth to get a good position." Therefore, concluded the professor,
while he would do his utmost to help, "I cannot help feeling that
the chances are going to be greatly against you." Deeply hurt, Lewisohn wrote years later that Carpenter had "a very keen tribal instinct of the self-protective sort and felt in [Lewisohn] the
implacable foe of the New England dominance over our national
life."[19]

In 1906 he left Columbia before receiving his doctorate. In the
same year, Ludwig married Mary Arnold Crocker Childs. Mrs.
Childs, English-born, was a divorcée, a mother of four, and at least

[17]Lewisohn, "Books We Have Made," Charleston *Sunday News and Courier*,
1903, 12 July 1918.

[18]Carl Van Doren, "William Gilmore Simms," in *Dictionary of American Biography*, ed. Dumas Malone (New York NY, 1946) 17: 174.

[19]*Up Stream*, 140-43.

seventeen years his senior. According to a cousin of Ludwig, in an interview with Stanley Chyet in 1958, she was "a most charming woman and very brilliant, much too old for Ludwig. She was a grandmother when she married Ludwig, who was then twenty-three years old."[20]

To say that this was a Freudian slip is to describe their relationship. Within a few years, as early as Lewisohn's first novel, *The Broken Snare*, written in Charleston between 1906 and 1908, it was clear that he had already discovered himself and was no longer content to be married to his "mother." The fact that she would not give Ludwig a divorce until almost thirty years later, when she was probably seventy or so, is the key to almost all of his novels and his preoccupation with the problems of marriage, sex, and disparate ages between partners.

After seeking a position in literature in a score of universities and being refused because of his "race," Ludwig was offered a job in the German department of the University of Wisconsin. A year later, because of the economic needs of his family, he moved to Ohio State University. In Columbus, he wrote *The Modern Drama*, *The Spirit of Modern German Literature*, *The Poets of Modern France*, and began the autobiographical chronicle, *Up Stream*.

Lewisohn's *The Broken Snare*, written in the two years after his departure from Columbia University, was published in 1908. Brutally rejected by the Charleston *News and Courier* as "profoundly disgusting," a story "reeking with the sweat of the vulgarest human passions," the novel was a rather well told story about a young woman's attempts to find herself by running off with a man.[21] Set in Charleston, where the aristocracy was already beginning to decay, there was in the book "a sense, shadowy and inarticulate, but deep enough, of our homelessness in the universe, of our terrible helplessness before it." In *Up Stream*, having chosen to articulate honestly his American experience, he wrote that to him, "Life was ugly and mean and, above all things, false in its assumptions and

---

[20]Cora H. Evans to Stanley Chyet, June 1958, in Chyet, "Ludwig Lewisohn," 141, n. 22.

[21]*Up Stream*, 169; see also Adolph Gillis, *Ludwig Lewisohn: The Artist and His Message* (New York NY, 1933) 27-28.

measures." He knew that the "notion of liberty," so precious a
word to Americans, was no longer alive, if it had ever been, for the
unassimilated foreigner.[22]

It was in *Up Stream* that Lewisohn demonstrated the courage
that had come to him during those years in a hostile environment
in Columbus, Ohio. Married to a woman from whom he was already desperately running, he discovered that he was at heart a he-
retic and a rebel yearning to be free. He felt that if only we all told
each other the naked, if devastating, truth, we might master life.
His yearning, reflected in *The Broken Snare* and *Up Stream*, was the
desire to become a free spirit. This he described explicitly in *Don
Juan* (1923), written after Ludwig ran off to Paris with Thelma
Spear, a half-Jewish would-be singer who was twenty years his junior. Although he did get a Mexican divorce from Mary, it was not
recognized in the United States, so escape to Europe was one way
to freedom. In *The Case of Mr. Crump* (1926) he describes how his
hero, a Southern Christian musician, after being wrongly vilified as
a Jew, followed by his wife's detectives, and enduring unbearable
constraints, kills his wife with a fireplace poker. At the price of freedom, he had won his freedom.

Between 1916 and 1921, Lewisohn realized that "so long as there
is discrimination, there is exile."[23] At that time he prophesied that
unless America "abandons its duality of conscience, unless it
learns to honor and practice a stronger spiritual veracity, it will
either destroy civilization through disasters yet unheard of or sink
into a memory and into a shadow of a name."[24] Ironically, it was in
World War I, the war "to make the world safe for democracy," that
a mob psychology and a passion for sacrifice emerged. In spite of
his passionate Americanness, he was seen as "good, loyal Southerners—guardians of Christianity, morality, and democracy—regard a 'nigger-lover.'"[25] In place of the notion of liberty, there was
intolerance. Assimilation to what was now a burning question.

---

[22]*The Broken Snare*, 140, and *Up Stream*, 171, 281-84.

[23]*Up Stream*, 144.

[24]Ibid., 148.

[25]Ibid., 245.

In 1908, in *The Broken Snare*, Lewisohn had just begun to grope for a free, spiritually rewarding life. After 1923 it became possible for him to be more open and courageous than he had been from 1916 to 1922 with a despised and vindictive wife beside him. With the publication of book after book, Lewisohn departed more and more from the South; New York became his favorite locality. Meanwhile, having publicly proclaimed his return to a Judaism he had never known, the conflict between a creative free spirit and a wife who seemed to live only to keep him on a chain became the passion that forced his novels into being.

In *The World of Our Fathers*, Irving Howe contends that in both Southern and Jewish writers, "A subculture finds its voice and its passion at exactly the moment it approaches disintegration." It was Lewisohn's fate to be both a Southerner and a Jew. As a Southerner he tried unsuccessfully to feed his soul on the astringent Protestantism of Charleston, South Carolina; as a Jew he passed from nonbeing to affirmation. As a man and a writer, maturing in the 1920s and 1930s, he announced his roots in both subcultures, even though in his personal life he suffered the pangs of multiple rejections. It was, on the one hand, what used to be called a classic case of unresolved Oedipal conflict in which his tight-knit, German-Jewish, Victorian family clashed with the loneliness, libidinal drives, and needs and errors of a freedom-seeking young man in New York. On the other hand, in a more modern interpretation, it was Lewisohn's adolescent need for autonomy and identity that impelled him through life. Smothered by his mother, he did not know who he was when he attended Columbia University. Married to Mary, a mother-substitute, he was still unable to find himself or be himself. The marriage, therefore, was a metaphor for what he experienced in his youth. The result was that Lewisohn, a neurotically driven and inhibited adult, sought spiritual, psychic, and emotional freedom in his books and in his women throughout his life. Midway through the 1930s, Mary finally gave Ludwig a divorce. He married twice more after his relationship with Thelma came to an end.

In 1948 he helped establish Brandeis University's English department, and in 1955, rich in experiences, honored for his creative work and commitment, he died. He had fought his way upward.

He had made a complete circle. Beginning in a world of books, enclosed in an Oedipal and separation pattern, he had found himself through a penetrating self-examination and a return to his roots. For Ludwig Lewisohn, a German-born, Charleston-bred, American-Jewish author, it had been a battle up the literary stream.

Contributors

HAROLD WECHSLER. Associate Professor of Education, Department of Education, University of Chicago. Author of a number of monographs and articles dealing with American education and the Holocaust.

DANIEL WALDEN. Professor of American Studies, Pennsylvania State University. Author of numerous books and articles in the field of American Jewish literature.

MYRON BERMAN. Rabbi, Congregation Beth-El, Richmond, Virginia. Author of several works and articles, among which is *Richmond's Jewry, 1769-1976* (1979).

DAVID MORGAN. Professor of History and Chairman, Department of Social Sciences, University of Montevallo. Author of a number of books and articles in American Colonial history.

LOUIS SCHMIER. Professor of History, Valdosta State College. Author of a number of books and articles in Southern Jewish History, among which is *Reflections on Southern Jewry* (1982).

JOHN McKAY SHEFTALL. Atlanta attorney. Author of several monographs and articles in the field of colonial Georgia history and genealogy.

SOLOMON BREIBART. Retired school teacher, historian for Congregation Beth Elohim, Charleston, South Carolina. Author of several articles dealing with Charleston's Jewry. President of Southern Jewish Historical Society.